Leadership Roles of Chief Academic Officers

David G. Brown, *Editor*

NEW DIRECTIONS FOR HIGHER EDUCATION
MARTIN KRAMER, *Editor-in-Chief*

Number 47, September 1984

Paperback sourcebooks in
The Jossey-Bass Higher Education Series

Jossey-Bass Inc., Publishers
San Francisco • Washington • London

David G. Brown (Ed.).
Leadership Roles of Chief Academic Officers.
New Directions for Higher Education, no. 47.
Volume XII, number 3.
San Francisco: Jossey-Bass, 1984.

New Directions for Higher Education Series
Martin Kramer, *Editor-in-Chief*

New Directions for Higher Education (publication number USPS
990-880) is published quarterly by Jossey-Bass Inc., Publishers.
New Directions is numbered sequentially — please order extra
copies by sequential number. The volume and issue numbers
above are included for the convenience of libraries. Second-class
postage rates paid at San Francisco, California, and at
additional mailing offices.

Correspondence:
Subscriptions, single-issue orders, change of address notices, undelivered
copies, and other correspondence should be sent to Subscriptions,
Jossey-Bass Inc., Publishers, 433 California Street, San Francisco,
California 94104.

Editorial correspondence should be sent to the Consulting Editor,
Martin Kramer, 2807 Shasta Road, Berkeley, California 94708.

Library of Congress Catalogue Card Number LC 83-82749

International Standard Serial Number ISSN 0271-0560

International Standard Book Number ISBN 87589-997-8

Cover art by Willi Baum

Manufactured in the United States of America

Ordering Information

The paperback sourcebooks listed below are published quarterly and can be ordered either by subscription or as single copies.

Subscriptions cost $35.00 per year for institutions, agencies, and libraries. Individuals can subscribe at the special rate of $25.00 per year *if payment is by personal check.* (Note that the full rate of $35.00 applies if payment is by institutional check, even if the subscription is designated for an individual.) Standing orders are accepted.

Single copies are available at $8.95 when payment accompanies order, and *all single-copy orders under $25.00 must include payment.* (California, Washington, D.C., New Jersey, and New York residents please include appropriate sales tax.) For billed orders, cost per copy is $8.95 plus postage and handling. (Prices subject to change without notice.)

Bulk orders (ten or more copies) of any individual sourcebook are available at the following discounted prices: 10–49 copies, $8.05 each; 50–100 copies, $7.15 each; over 100 copies, *inquire.* Sales tax and postage and handling charges apply as for single copy orders.

To ensure correct and prompt delivery, all orders must give either the *name of an individual* or an *official purchase order number.* Please submit your order as follows:

Subscriptions: specify series and subscription year.
Single Copies: specify sourcebook code and issue number (such as, HE8).

Mail orders for United States and Possessions, Latin America, Canada, Japan, Australia, and New Zealand to:
Jossey-Bass Inc., Publishers
433 California Street
San Francisco, California 94104

Mail orders for all other parts of the world to:
Jossey-Bass Limited
28 Banner Street
London EC1Y 8QE

New Directions for Higher Education Series
Martin Kramer, *Editor-in-Chief*

Contents

Editor's Notes

Best-sellers such as *In Search of Excellence* and *Megatrends* resonate to the themes of bold leadership, participatory decision making, and focused excellence. Today leadership counts; this is an era of choice. Bold choices may, and should, be made. Before when resources were scarce, great leaders like Eliot, Hutchins, and Rockefeller also made bold choices. Today the resources are still scarce, but the choices — and information about them — are manifold. Decisions involve simultaneously choosing where to contract and where to expand. They must be made in the open, and their consequences are more easily traced today through masses of newly available data.

This past fall, I interviewed more than fifty college presidents. These interviews underscored the same theme: It is a time for choice, for boldness. Whatever this means for presidents, it is magnified many times over for chief academic officers (CAOs). Presidents have big chunks of nondiscretionary time; virtually all CAO time is discretionary, although it does not seem so. If we look at how different CAOs spend their time, we see that there is no standard schedule. Presidents must — but CAOs may — relate to the board, act as figureheads, and preside at commencement. Some CAOs spend 60 percent of their time raising money at foundations; some never leave campus. Some spend half their time counseling students; some see students only in groups, and only about student government matters. The position of CAOs is defined by its occupant. In these times, the CAO at most institutions will spend time deciding the future of the college or university, but the procedures of the CAO clearly will not be those used by the institution builders of the late nineteenth century, since today's wisest decisions seem to come from teams.

In its conception, this volume is very practical. It is probably best read while the reader is overloaded with planning tasks and in the midst of framing an agenda for the next several years. In fact, it is a compilation of thought stimulators — issues are raised, solutions pursued, questions are asked, whys and whats and what ifs, achievements, and dreams are explored. Its concepts are addressed to the chief academic officer, but are equally applicable to the work of college deans (and, in most instances, department chairs), and are presented in the

1

hope that this volume will help academic leaders anticipate the future with wisdom and effective action. The assumption is that the reader is seeking stimulation — a thought catalyst — and that in-depth treatment of topics will require additional reading (generally of the literature cited after most chapters).

This volume begins with thirty-six aphorisms compiled by Glenn E. Brooks; our hope is that readers will apply them to evaluating and adjusting how they have defined the scope and opportunity of their jobs. It concludes with perspectives on the future. In Chapter Nine, Maurice Glicksman gives his views about where academia is heading and how it is likely to get there. And, as an example of courageous and comprehensive planning, the recommendations of Notre Dame's Committee on Priorities and Commitments for Excellence are highlighted by Timothy O'Meara in Chapter Ten. The real conclusion of this volume, however, should be the reader's personal sketch of what actions he or she might wisely take in the next several years; otherwise, this sourcebook will have failed to achieve its full intended purpose.

Between these attempts to conceive the CAO's job and the college's future are chapters dealing with specific issues and methods. Robert E. Wolverton describes the CAO's need for perspicacity in Chapter Two. As mechanisms for enabling improvements, Christine A. Young discusses the budget (Chapter Seven), J. Terrence Kelly and Kamala Anandam prospect the theory and practice of computer technology (Chapter Eight), and William J. Hynes (Chapter Four) and John Oppelt (Chapter Five) examine means of effecting change through faculty leadership via faculty development. Throughout this volume, each author somehow touches on the themes of openness in decision making, participation, and involvement. Highlighted in the discussion of reallocation by Kenneth P. Mortimer and Annette C. Caruso (Chapter Six), these themes are put under the microscope by W. Edmund Moomaw in his discussion of participatory leadership strategy (Chapter Three).

All the chapters have a common goal: to start each reader on longer-term and broader-scale thinking about his or her leadership task.

David G. Brown
Editor

*David G. Brown served as a chief academic officer for fifteen
years, first at Drake University and later at Miami
University. He is now chancellor of the University of North
Carolina at Asheville.*

Quick phrases often hold deep meanings. Glenn Brooks asked thirteen chief academic officers and deans, "If you had several items of advice for our new colleagues, what would they be?"

Aphorisms and Maxims for Chief Academic Officers

Glenn E. Brooks

1. Ask "What will a given decision mean in five years?"
2. Let the president and faculty busy themselves with your agenda.
3. All effort at long-range planning will be attended by a steady series of ephemeral crises, deflections, and catastrophes, but it must be done.
4. The role of the dean, finally, is to enable faculty to do better, more effectively, more efficiently, and with fewer interruptions the thing that they do best.
5. Don't compromise on what you consider important in the long range for what others might consider urgent in the short range.
6. Don't try to change too many things at once.
7. Teach a course occasionally. To do it regularly is too much of an imposition on the students, but its effect on you is important.

The interview respondents were Keith O. Anderson (St. Olaf College), Theodore S. Baker (University of New England), Joan P. Bean (Fairleigh Dickinson University), Zeddie Bowen (College of William and Mary), Robert Lewis (Cornell College), Anthony Lisska (Denison University), Robert M. Longsworth (Oberlin College), Douglas Northrop (Ripon College), David Potter (Haverford College), Jack E. Rossman (Macalester College), Patsy H. Sampson (Drake University), Robert T. Voelkel (Pomona College), and Frank F. Wong (Beloit College).

D. G. Brown (Ed.). *Leadership Roles of Chief Academic Officers.* New Directions for Higher Education, no. 47. San Francisco: Jossey-Bass, September 1984.

8. Deans are hired for their ideas and credentials, but retained for their stamina and ability to help the faculty and the staff get along with each other.
9. Money more often masks problems than solves them.
10. Presidents cannot know all that they must appear to understand; they depend on deans to keep them connected to and credible within their institutions.
11. Listen a lot. Keep your mouth shut unless you really want to say something.
12. Reserve categorical statements to the big issues, such as liberal arts mission, commitment, and professionalism.
13. Forced decisions are costly. Use them only in emergencies.
14. Keep your staff small. Be at least as tough with authorizing expenditures in your administration as with requests from other areas.
15. The pat on the back is better than the exhortation to do better. Congratulate your faculty and staff on their accomplishments.
16. New ideas for academic development need tending and faculty sponsorship for legitimacy. Plant them as seeds with care, see to their nurture unobtrusively, and take only inner pride in their flowering.
17. Communicate about problems rather than solutions. If others can be persuaded that a problem exists, solutions will follow.
18. Be open with colleagues. Rumors are almost always worse than the realities.
19. Ideas beyond institutional means are not pipe dreams, but the stuff of grant proposals.
20. A difference in material makes a material difference — in students, faculty, and staff.
21. It is easier to touch bases than to mend fences.
22. Never surprise the president.
23. Be wary of all individuals claiming to speak for the whole faculty.
24. Hang out around all natural gathering places.
25. Be meticulous about confidentiality.
26. Manage appointments; don't let them manage you.
27. Don't play favorites.
28. Keep a log of discussions that take place in your office, especially regarding personal matters.
29. Be available to the faculty always, and to students when they need to talk.
30. Confidants are essential but should not be sought within the faculty or staff.

31. Write in pencil and carry a big eraser.
32. Feeding intellectual roots—through teaching, research, or focused reading—is as important for administrators as for faculty members.
33. Colleges are both hierarchically structured and collegially based. Deans alone must live in both worlds simultaneously.
34. Don't forget that the kitchen is normally hot.
35. No matter how much you may be upset, do not use your office to make retribution.
36. Don't give up your tenure.

Glenn E. Brooks is dean of Colorado College.

From moment to moment, the chief academic officer (CAO)
must be prepared to deal with a bewildering variety of
developing relationships, priorities, problems, and potentials.

The Chief Academic Officer: Argus on the Campus

Robert E. Wolverton

Every chief academic officer (CAO) wears many hats and often views
developments with alarm. A CAO who looks around his or her position
within the institution must have these views: (1) up, to the chief executive officer (CEO) and the governing board; (2) down, to deans and
others who report to the CAO; (3) sideways, to institutional peers with
responsibilities in student, financial, administrative, development, and
other affairs; and (4) oblique, to those with such titles as associate and
assistant vice-president, associate and assistant dean, and assistant to
the president. At the same time, the CAO must take a campus view of
faculty, students, and curricula; a system view to answer queries on
such subjects as duplication of programs, tenure and academic freedom, the quality of students, and the mission of this institution as
opposed to that of others in the system; and a national view to be aware
of new concerns and issues within the profession in other parts of the
country. Finally, for their own sense of survival and well-being, CAOs
must occasionally have a review of where they are going, what they are
doing, and what they are becoming.

D. G. Brown (Ed.). *Leadership Roles of Chief Academic Officers.* New Directions
for Higher Education, no. 47. San Francisco: Jossey-Bass, September 1984.

All this viewing requires, figuratively, that the CAO have multiple eyes, some of which are awake at any given moment. Thus, the most apt symbol for the CAO is the mythological Argus Panoptes ("all-seeing"), the powerful giant with a hundred eyes, only two of which slept at a time. The only time when all Argus' eyes were asleep, lulled by the beautiful singing of the god Hermes, Hermes killed him. His eyes were taken by Hera, the wife of Zeus, and put into the tail of her favored bird, the peacock. The CAO, then, like Argus, must have clear and open eyes, for on the CAO's views rest the quality and the reputation of the institution, as well as the satisfaction of students, faculty, and other administrators.

The various kinds of viewing done by the CAO reflect a series of obvious and subtle relationships that exist on campus. To the extent that the CAO can focus accurately and simultaneously on everything and make necessary adjustments as relationships and people change, he or she will be successful. It will be instructive, therefore, to investigate these several relationships through the eyes of the Argus on the campus.

1. The View Up. On every campus, the CAO is both an A (has reporting subordinates or colleagues) and a B (reports to someone, normally the CEO). Within the usual organizational structure, the CEO is also an A (with vice-officers and others reporting) and a B (reports to the governing board). There is a defined system of accountability within which most administrators at all levels feel quite comfortable; without an A to whom they report, most Bs (who must also function as As) would feel, to some degree, directionless. The CAO, then, in the role of B, views up, to the CEO, expecting to receive responsibility, authority, and rewards in return for being a leader (as A) and a follower (as B). It is absolutely imperative that the parties to this relationship — CAO (B) and CEO (A) — be in philosophical and pragmatic agreement at least 80 to 85 percent of the time. Agreement to a level of more than 90 percent could result in a real or perceived "yes-man" relationship of CAO to CEO, while agreement below the level of 80 percent could result in tensions and stresses, with negative impact on the B–A relationship and on many others within the institution. The CAO, looking up, must find an A with whom there can be mutual trust, reliance, and, at times, disagreement; the two of them, however, must share the mission, goals, and objectives of their common institution and must work cooperatively to fulfill them. In doing so, they should genuinely enjoy their professional relationship. If their professional relationship is enjoyable, quite possibly their personal relationship will also be positive and enjoyable, and from the strong relationship of this A and this B the campus itself may reflect a cooperative and dynamic spirit.

To build a strong, positive, and enjoyable relationship, two essential ingredients are required: almost daily interaction, and time. With its frequent and close interaction over a period of months and years, the CAO–CEO relationship resembles that of a good marriage, in which both verbal and nonverbal communication occurs and in which respect and trust ovecome irritations and problems. Irritations and problems do attend CAO–CEO relationships, particularly because of the different constituent groups each partner normally deals with. The CEO must be alert to governing board members, legislators and other elected and appointed officials, alumni, and the nonacademic administrative officers of the institution, while the CAO must be alert to subordinate deans and directors, faculty, students, and other administrators whose offices affect faculty and students and the total learning environment. Thus, the perceptions picked up by the CEO may be more external, while those gained by the CAO are more internal. The task of pulling these different perceptions together, having them meet on the same plane, and ending with a harmonious and commonly understood decision or action calls forth the best and continuing efforts of both the CEO and the CAO.

A most troublesome aspect of any CAO–CEO relationship concerns what the CEO should know, when, and for what purpose. On the one hand, the CEO should not have to be overburdened with information but, on the other hand, the CEO also should not be caught "off base" and embarrassed by a lack of information. Here, again, it is helpful for the CAO and CEO to have some generally agreed-upon system of what needs to be communicated, when, and for what possible purpose. Both must realize, however, that no plan will be foolproof, for it is impossible to predict who may ask what of the CEO in a given circumstance.

2. The View Down. Now that the CAO has been (briefly) depicted as a B (reporting to the CEO), it is proper to depict the CAO as an A (supervising those who report). As the A responsible for the academic life of the college or university, the CAO must be part detective, part judge, and a two-way effective communicator, interpreter, and advocate. The CAO must diplomatically and candidly reflect the goals, objectives, and needs of the CEO, of the governing body, and of other valid and timely constituent voices and at the same time reflect the goals, objectives, and needs of faculty, students, and subordinates. With all these efforts to communicate, interpret, and advocate, the CAO must also maintain integrity and credibility with all those who depend on his or her judgments, decisions, and actions. How can one be one's own person and also be everyone else's? No one ever said it would be easy.

As detective and judge, the CAO hears, reads, and responds to numerous requests or expectations, all with one common denominator — namely, that each is considered the top priority by the petitioning individual or group. Establishing priorities in budgets, personnel, or programs, the CAO will inevitably make someone angry or at least frustrated. Still, it is the CAO's responsibility, and he or she must be able to say no firmly and fairly: Limited resources, changing student and parent curricular demands, faculty tenure ratios, new admission and graduation requirements set by off-campus and well-intentioned critics, and many other factors over which there is little or no control will not allow the CAO to please all the people all the time. In spite of the problems, however, the CAO, as A to various Bs, must remain relentlessly optimistic and only as infrequently as necessary view developments with alarm. It may help the CAO to enter a private closet periodically and emit his or her own howls of frustration.

Finally, just as it is important for the CAO and the CEO to establish and maintain a strong, positive, and enjoyable relationship, so it is important for the CAO to create similar relationships with Bs. Frequent meetings and day-to-day interactions over time will make the CAO a more effective A, better able to sort out facts and perceptions, evaluate Bs, and have their confidence and support.

3. The View Sideways. Thus far, the Argus-eyed CAO has been viewed in the roles of B to the CEO and A to subordinates. As the academic leader, the CAO must look at times to see what positive changes may be called for or what faculty or student problems must be addressed. Often, in addressing particular problems, the CAO must view sideways and gain the assistance of those in peer positions — vice-presidents or deans for student affairs, business and financial affairs, or administration. A student's nonpayment of tuition and a faculty member's nonpayment of parking tickets both involve the CAO, even though the CAO may not have the authority to act. In such cases, the peer colleague must act and should keep the CAO notified, particularly if the case is settled. The sideways view of the CAO, far from being suspicious, is necessary, so that all who report to the CEO know where the problems are or may be and can solicit each other's advice or assistance. The CEO may wish to have regular weekly meetings with Bs, or these Bs may wish to meet regularly together themselves to ensure that all know what they need to know or to share common concerns or interests.

Because of the sideways view, as well as relationships among those who are Bs to the CEO and As to their own subordinates, between CAOs and their peers there is not the same sort of accountability or close working arrangement found between an A and a B. Nevertheless, for the best interests of the individuals and the campus, the relationships should be amicable and trusting, so that a team spirit is engendered and maintained. In this age of specialized knowledge and skills, there must be broad-based reliance on the judgment and competence of the administrators who form the executive team. The executives may be thought of as a rowing team; progress is certainly hampered if six rowers are rowing furiously in one direction and the seventh is rowing furiously in the opposite direction.

4. The Oblique View. For a variety of reasons — because of the need for specialists, or to shorten the span of control of an A, or to preclude the possibility of creating an "indispensable" person — a type of administrator may appear, bearing the title of "assistant/associate to," "special assistant to," or "assistant/associate vice-president/dean." For these somewhat anomalous officers, the CAO must exercise the view oblique, that is, neither up nor down nor sideways. The CAO's own "assistant/associate (to)" may be treated as a B with no subordinates or may be an A – , with some who had earlier reported to the CAO still reporting to the *office* of A but not directly to A. Whatever the case, the CAO (A) and the A – or B must have an understood working arrangement, with frequent conversations about any possible redelegation of assignments, duties, and personnel.

The CAO's oblique view to the CEO's "assistant/associate (to)" may prove confusing, if not difficult. Although the CEO and the CEO's A – may have an understood working arrangement, the A – may try to speak for or represent the CEO without any such authority. In these instances, again, the CAO must call upon diplomatic skill and the special relationship with the CEO to clear the air and clarify the working arrangements. Even then, the CEO's A – may be perceived by the CAO as meddling if the A – continues to offer the CAO gratuitous advice or goes around the CAO and works with deans or others who report to the CAO. Since there is such potential for conscious or unconscious mischief, relationships among these administrators must be monitored more closely than those between a typical A and B.

Our discussion so far has suggested that the CAO, being Argus-like, views professional colleagues on campus in at least four ways — up, down, sideways, and oblique. Whether the organizational structure is pictured as a hierarchical pyramid or as a series of circles, the CAO has a superior, subordinates, peers, and frequently assistants or associates, all of whom must be worked with for the good of the college or university. If the mission, goals, and objectives of the institution are well known and agreed on by the administrative team, then the chances are good that the CAO, with the other administrators, will be successful. Still, there are impediments to be wary of, impediments that can strain or shatter working relationships without anyone's being at fault. Consider these hazards, for example: (1) the administrators may come from differing academic or nonacademic positions or disciplines, may have arrived at different times on campus, may have had no previous administrative experience, and are trying to become a new team with a new system of communication; (2) communication in English consists of some 750,000 words, supplemented by some 720,000 body and facial movements; (3) as the Italian economist Graicunas pointed out (in a formula named for him), given a situation with one A and ten Bs, 5,210 possible lines of communication exist; and (4) surprsie, the enemy of planning, can come from any quarter at any time, causing priorities to be quickly reordered. Considering all these impediments, the cliché may well be true: "We have a problem in communication." We are, indeed, far from equalling what some call the most effective and efficient system of communication in our society: the one used in professional football when within a period of thirty seconds, the quarterback calls the play, all eleven players know where to go and what to do, and the play is executed. Although the CAO may not equal the football quarterback, he or she certainly is one of the real "play makers," a team leader who must know what is being done, by whom, and for what purpose. To keep up with the surrounding world, the CAO must be Argus-eyed, serving as a reliable B to the CEO and a reliable A to several Bs.

To fulfill the roles of A (leader) and B (follower), the CAO does require some special gifts, skills, or natural bents. The more successful CAOs show these elements in common:

- Some period as a full-time faculty member, working "in the trenches" as teacher, adviser, researcher, committee member, and servant to the campus, society, or the professional field

- Previous administrative experience, particularly in a position requiring supervision of a budget and personnel
- Such personal traits as sensitivity to others, patience, integrity, courage, and a sense of humor
- Such acquired skills as listening well, knowing when to give up the fight, and understanding the total academic community so that synergy can result from the blend of available people and programs
- Wisdom, gained from formal and informal education, to make judgments that will attract consensus and yet allow for serendipity
- Optimism and idealism in equal measure, with decision-making and problem-solving abilities for a programmatic nature
- A desire to lead and serve others to the best of one's abilities and skills, and the realization that bouquets of thanks are much rarer than brickbats of complaints, and that today's problem was yesterday's solution to a problem.

In short, CAOs must be competent and motivated and must know themselves as well as knowing others and how to motivate, evaluate, and, if necessary, terminate them in humane and positive ways. CAOs have learned by being and by doing, and they have better than average understanding of the people as well as the programs for which the CAO has responsibility, authority, and accountability. And, having become CAOs, they continue to grow personally and professionally while at the same time assisting Bs in their development and growth.

In addition to the care, feeding, and viewing of personal working relationships, the CAO has certain other responsibilities demanding nearly constant viewing. First among these is the view of the academic health of the entire campus:

- Are there "soft spots" in the curriculum?
- Are faculty productive and satisfied?
- Are students properly challenged or, alternatively, taught basic knowledge needed for further progress?
- Are accrediting bodies positive in their assessments of quality?
- Are parents comfortable with the sort of education their children are receiving?
- Are funding agencies pleased with continuing research and its results?

- Are alumni encouraging their children and others to attend this institution because of its academic programs and quality?
- Are support services helping to create an atmosphere in which students can strive to reach their full potential?
- Is the library able to accommodate faculty and student demands? Is the computing center?
- Are stories of interest involving faculty or students finding their way into appropriate publications and nonprint media?
- Is the campus bookstore stocking books students can read with profit?
- Are the institution's graduates able to find jobs in keeping with their educational attainments or to attend the graduate schools of their choice?
- What is the faculty senate now considering, without any consultation with this office?

These questions and hundreds of others occur or reoccur to the CAO as he or she ponders the institution's mission, goals, and objectives and how they are being accomplished through the programs and activities on campus. The CAO's hundred eyes must be matched by a hundred ears as most of working time is spent in meetings — viewing, listening, nodding wisely, responding, and sharing the joys, expectations, disappointments, and questions of others. Then there is the paper blizzard that seems to blanket the office each day: reports, letters, memoranda, computer printouts, reprints of articles, tidbits torn from newspapers and magazines. And, the CAO muses, "All the time-management experts say to handle every piece of paper only once — ha!"

As parts of the campus view, there is also the CAO's attendance at such diverse affairs as sports events, faculty and student recitals, concerts and plays, art exhibits, evenings in student residence halls, and assorted receptions, teas, and programs whose purposes range from honoring the service of faculty and staff to welcoming a visiting group. Participation in such affairs is not mandatory, but an occasional appearance allows an audience to appreciate the CAO's visibility. Among other duties not found in the job description of the CAO is that of cheerleader for academic and nonacademic activities.

If the CAO's campus is officially part of a statewide system, or even if it is only one of a number of state-supported or state-assisted institutions, then the CAO must be aware of and often respond to the concerns of the governing board, parents, legislators, governmental leaders, such voices of influence as prominent newspapers or "movers and shakers," and pressure groups of every stripe. Whether the issue is the faculty's having to sign a loyalty oath, a concern that "free enterprise" be taught in the schools, questions about the research being done by particular faculty members, students demanding more "power" and "relevance," the rights of gay members of the campus, tenure and academic freedom, high salaries and perceived low work load, the quality of prospective teachers, or the lack of "basic skills" among recent graduates, the CAO must be prepared to respond in a civil and positive way. In time, the CAO finds that there is an annual and often a monthly issue or crisis demanding immediate attention, not only on the part of the individual institution but also on the part of all the state-supported institutions. One constant and continual struggle is that of acquiring necessary funds—state, student, and off-campus—to support the teaching, research, and service efforts of faculty and staff. The first surprise to the new CAO is, of course, that issues emerge in such quantity, with such swiftness, and from so many different sources. The telephone is a most useful tool for talking with other CAOs in the state and trying to build a collective response. A second surprise is that the CAO's own faculty often are not aware of certain issues or crises; thus, the CAO cannot tell the faculty daily, weekly, or monthly, "This is what I've done for you lately." The satisfaction of minor successes is often shared only with other CAOs, the president, and a spouse.

At the national level, too, there are issues that elicit the interest and response of an active CAO. The apathy of students in the fifties, the "baby boom" and the student unrest of the sixties and the seventies, changing educational priorities within federal agencies, current demographic data, economic outlook, the return to the basics, and the general education curricula of the eighties reflect the public's concern, dismay, and demands for action. At the same time, there are internal issues of national import: an expanding cadre of doctoral-degree recipients and a shrinking university teaching market in some fields; rapid growth in other fields, for which a very limited number of doctorates is available for the teaching slots; an advancing retirement age for faculty; loss of mobility for all the best or most fortunate faculty members; and post-tenure evaluations. These issues are equally demanding of considered thought and prudent action. The vast number of recent "report cards" on American education cannot be ignored by CAOs, who must now begin to forge alliances between secondary schools and their own campuses and find answers to such problems as the severe shortage of teachers in mathematics and the sciences or high school graduates who are underprepared for college. Again, certain peril awaits the CAO who is ignorant of or unresponsive to these national issues and their potential impact. Thus, attendance at national and regional professional meetings and subscription to appropriate books, journals, and periodicals really are "musts," even though they may be regarded as useless or as frills by the public and by state legislatures.

How can a CAO be taught the Argus-like vision required for the local, state, and national scenes? In truth, the vision cannot be taught; the CEO can only learn. Experience, a willingness to spend untold hours in learning and borrowing the experience and perceptions of others, and the fortitude to keep on trying against all obstacles certainly represent key factors in the CAO's acquiring the essential vision.

Given all the activities, attitudes, behaviors, and actions included in the CAO's official and unofficial job description, when, if at all, should the CAO decide to "hang it up" and move on to other positions and opportunities? Obviously, there is no magic time or set number of years of service. It is reasonable to suggest, however, that an annual review of one's total status as the CAO is in order. Such questions as these should be asked and answered truthfully: Am I doing what I want to be doing? Am I going where I want to be going? Am I becoming what I want to become? Am I effective in my working relationships with superiors, peers, and subordinates? Is my mental or physical health undergoing stress, burnout, or exhaustion? Am I doing anything remotely creative or innovative, or am I following routines requiring little imagination or growth? Is there a position, either in this university or another, where my contribution could be more beneficial to more people? Have I accomplished all the goals and objectives to which I subscribed last year? An annual appraisal conducted with oneself and one's colleagues will go far in helping a decision of whether to continue as the CAO. The one unquenchable truth, the truth to be recognized always, is that no one has a gun to the CAO's head saying, "You must be or remain the chief academic officer." It is up to the CAO to remember that truth, just as he or she must also remember that it is possible for all the Argus eyes to be lulled to sleep—by self-satisfaction, excessive praise, the feeling of indispensability, sheer ignorance, or apathy. Being lulled to sleep by any or all of these can, will, and should result—figuratively, of course—in the same fate as that experienced by the original Argus.

In summary, the CAO in every institution of higher education has a unique role: to lead, administer, and manage the people and ideas that are the lifeblood of the institution. The position of CAO certainly is indispensable, although those who hold the position are not. In filling that position, the CAO must recognize his or her own personal and professional strengths and weaknesses and use the talents of others to complement or compensate for them. To say that the position offers challenges is an understatement, but to say that the job cannot be adequately handled is an overstatement. As a member of an administrative team of competent and caring individuals, the Argus-eyed CAO makes a major contribution to the campus and all its concerned constituencies. Recognizing that contribution may be reward enough for a CAO who has voluntarily forsaken the noble profession of teaching for an equally noble profession: serving a larger, more varied, and more demanding audience.

References

Burns, G. P. (Ed.). *Administrators in Higher Education: Their Functions and Coordination.* New York: Harper & Row, 1962.
Cohen, M. D., and March, J. G. *Leadership and Ambiguity.* New York: McGraw-Hill, 1974.
Dyer, F. C., and Dyer, J. M. *The Enjoyment of Management.* Homewood, Ill.: Dow Jones-Irwin, 1971.
Eble, K. E. *The Art of Administration.* San Francisco: Jossey-Bass, 1978.
Walker, D. E. *The Effective Administrator.* San Francisco: Jossey-Bass, 1979.

Robert E. Wolverton is vice-president for academic affairs at Mississippi State University.

The chief academic officer must know how to initiate
a process of change.

Participatory Leadership Strategy

W. Edmund Moomaw

Asked once to describe the powers of the presidency, President Truman replied, "I sit here all day trying to persuade people to do what they ought to have sense enough to do without my persuading them. That's all the power of the presidency amounts to" (Neustadt, 1958). Defining leadership as the power of persuasion, Neustadt's book, *Presidential Power,* describes the tools and influences available to the president of the United States to "persuade" people to do what the president wants—and what the president can do to those who are not persuaded. Peters and Waterman, in their recent work on management in American business, *In Search of Excellence: Lessons from America's Best-Run Companies* (1982), discuss three variables of leadership—pathfinding, decision making, and implementation. They found that traditional leaders are good at decision making but weak in the other two areas, both of which they see as essential to effective and successful leadership.

Leadership in the academic community differs from that in government and business in two important respects: the nature of those whom we seek to lead, primarily our faculties; and the nature of the academic enterprise itself. Faculty members are more complex than voters, who periodically determine who holds power, and employees,

D. G. Brown (Ed.). *Leadership Roles of Chief Academic Officers.* New Directions
for Higher Education, no. 47. San Francisco: Jossey-Bass, September 1984.

who pursue profits. Faculty are highly educated, independent professionals trained to question and be critical, and dedicated to modeling for others those same qualities. Faculty have their own ideas about their profession, as well as a natural and sometimes healthy skepticism about alternative proposals. Unlike the proverbial horse, they often can neither be led to water nor made to drink it.

The nature of colleges and universities is not to seek popular approval and profits above all else. We see our roles as seeking the truth, wherever we may find it, and we trust that others will judge this search for knowledge important for its own sake. Increasingly, however, external forces and social changes have brought pressures on the traditional autonomy and tranquility of our campuses, creating anew the need for sound leadership. In some ways this need for effective leadership presents the paradox of, on the one hand, the desire for swift and tough decisions to respond to today's rapidly changing society and, on the other, the desire for openness and widespread involvement in academic governance. With the goal of developing a leadership model that will achieve both of these objectives, we turn to an examination of two approaches to academic leadership.

The Bureaucratic Model

Many institutions seem by default to develop the *bureaucratic model* of administrative leadership. Centralized decisions tend to result when there are strong outside pressures on the institution, such as enrollment and financial pressures, and when difficult circumstances need to be faced. Problems are defined and resolved at the top, with little consultation within the institution. Both paperwork and the bureaucracy needed to administer it increase in size, while hassling and internal conflict grow, little responsibility is delegated, and long-range planning is usually displaced by managing crises. This approach to leadership is usually a very formal one with clear organizational divisions. There probably are many persons who report directly to the CAO, with the result that there is little time for the CAO to do anything else but respond to their questions or to issues they may raise. Because the CAO maintains tight control over all decisions, even those dealing with daily operational matters, subordinates are unwilling to take action without approval, and they hesitate to make suggestions. Strict control of the budget is a particular characteristic of the academic bureaucratic model. Individual departments may be budgeted certain amounts for travel, supplies, and the like, but the bureaucratic leader will require advance approval of specific plans and probably will want a host of forms completed before the expenditures can be made. Because there are few incentives, and because people are not trusted to exercise independent responsibility, few suggestions or initiatives develop.

Peters and Waterman (1982) call this approach to leadership in business the *rational model.* In this model, the leader's task is to keep things tidy and under control and to ensure that every possible contingency is accounted for. Rational leaders issue orders, make black-and-white decisions, and treat people as factors of production. Most important, leaders in the national model place their emphases not on people but on money, machines, and control.

The weaknesses of the bureaucratic model of leadership in education and the rational model of leadership in business are similar. By placing emphasis on making swift and tough decisions in a controlled environment, leaders in these models omit what Peters and Waterman (1982) refer to as the pathfinding and implementation steps. They miss thereby the benefits of innovation and experimentation, benefits that come from involving more people in the process and in having a more informal, less controlled environment. The bureaucratic leader's criticisms or suggestions create inflexibility. Most unfortunately, perhaps, the bureaucratic style leads to distrust and low morale within the faculty and staff, as well as to a lessening of the institution's ability to meet new challenges creatively and cooperatively. The bureaucratic leader can control the institution, but this style of leadership does not motivate the faculty and the staff, who must approve or at least implement new programs and other changes if they are to be successful. Another leadership style is needed.

The Participation Model

The *participation model* of academic leadership is characterized by open information on campus, a clearly focused and shared mission, widespread delegation and acceptance of responsibility, broad involvement in policy formulation, clear evaluation procedures, and rewards for those who do well. This model advances the concept that people tend to be most enthusiastic and most productive in their activities when they have a voice in what is happening to them and to their programs. This concept does not mean that people want to take over the institution or that the leadership must surrender its overall responsibility. It suggests instead the value of leaders who are aware that the people in an organization are most important to institutional creativity, problem solving, and new program implementation and that a system of decentralized leadership is most likely to ensure the needed high level of motivation. It means also that leaders must listen to ideas from faculty and staff members, trusting and having confidence in those who present ideas. If leaders maintain a climate of open information and give attention to faculty and staff development, this trust and confidence will not be misplaced.

The participation model does not mean a completely open and democratic system of leadership; absolute democracy will not work as a model for academic leadership. For the participation leadership model to be successful, the leader must know which activities to centralize and keep under control and which activities to decentralize and place beyond direct control. In general, the most workable guiding principle is that broad statements of mission and goals, evaluation procedures, and leadership training should be centralized, while the leader should decentralize the managing of daily activities, proposals and planning for meeting the mission and goals, and proposals and planning for solving problems. The academic leader will be most likely to be successful if five important principles are kept in mind.

Five Principles of Academic Leadership in the Participation Model

1. Articulating Mission and Goals. Every college and university must have an academic mission, and it is a key responsibility of the CAO to articulate this mission and the broad goals of the academic program. Emphasis on mission and goals causes people to recommit themselves to those goals and examine their own activities in light of them. Moreover, continuous articulation of mission and goals will have the effect of making them the conventional wisdom. Emphasis on the broad goals of education is particularly effective when the faculty is considering revisions of significant parts of the curriculum, such as general education requirements. This emphasis will keep attention on the institution's long-range objectives rather than on short-term problems.

2. Developing a Leadership Team. One of the most important aspects of successful academic leadership is the development of a leadership team. This team can be particularly helpful with leadership's pathfinding and implementation components, to use

Peters and Waterman's (1982) terms. The leadership team is especially important in serving as the vehicle for decentralization of decision making. Responsibility for administration of daily details can be delegated to members of the leadership team. Team members should have clear responsibilities, adequate support, full informal access to the dean, and visible delegated authority to carry out responsibilities in their own ways within general policy.

Since good academic administrators are not born, perhaps the most important factor in building a successful leadership team is providing resources and opportunities for administrative training and development. Funds should be provided for attending workshops and other kinds of training activities. In addition, there must be funds for support services.

An important role for the leadership team can be that of a planning and support group for the academic program and the CAO. This role can be performed in either a formal or informal setting, in which ideas can be discussed openly and honestly. Criticism of ideas and actions can be made in a supporting and trusting atmosphere. The forum also can serve as an important means for the CAO to be informed about the faculty's opinions and the program's effectiveness. The leadership team can also communicate and interpret administrative views to the faculty.

At Birmingham–Southern College this academic leadership team was developed by consolidating twenty academic departments into six interdisciplinary academic divisions. This reorganization reduced from twenty-five to ten the number of persons who reported directly to the CAO. Responsibility for the day-to-day management of the instructional program was delegated to the division chairs, leaving the academic dean available for planning and evaluation activities. Each division chair was given a twelve-month contract and a reduced teaching load so that there would be time for the additional activities. Secretarial services also were provided for each chair. The divisional approach to a leadership team saves money because it avoids the need for a staff of assistants and associates in the CAO's office. As a group, the division chairs form an academic council that shares responsibility with the CAO for broad planning and evaluation activities. In addition to providing a more effective approach to leadership and management, the divisional system at Birmingham–Southern also facilitates more interdisciplinary, integrative, and synthesizing programs, as well as greater faculty participation in discussion of educational matters. The divisions form the basis of the academic governance structure, nominating and electing members to key faculty committees and initiating curricular changes.

3. Encouraging Broad Involvement in New Ideas. Two important ingredients of a vital educational program are a continuing infusion of new ideas into the institution and an awareness among faculty members that innovation is encouraged and supported. The ideal academic leader can be described as one who, upon seeing a faculty member fall to the ground after sawing off the wrong end of a tree limb, would help the faculty member to his feet and compliment him on his innovative spirit, encouraging him to continue the experiment. (The saw, needless to say, would have been purchased with an institutional faculty development grant, and released time would have been provided for the activity.)

The point of encouraging new ideas and innovation throughout the institution is that no one person or office has a monopoly on new approaches. Moreover, encouraging the broad development of ideas builds support for still other changes and programs when they come forward. Successful approaches for encouraging new ideas include a faculty development program, a sabbatical program, and the presentation of new ideas to the campus through outside guest speakers and availability of new books and articles. All these approaches cost money; but, compared to an academic program with little spirit and few new ideas, they are a bargain.

4. Evaluating. One of the most useful tools available to the CAO is evaluation of programs and other activities in the academic area. The CAO should be available to initiate such evaluations. Programs and activities should be evaluated against established goals and objectives. Evaluation provides opportunities for discussion of programs, for revision of goals, and for the generation of more new ideas. Frequent evaluations should take place not only for programs and activities but also for faculty and staff members. These evaluations should have constructive criticism and improvement as their purpose, and the process should culminate in a personal discussion between the faculty or staff member and the immediate superior. When done well, this process can build trusting relationships and motivation.

5. Using a Reward System. There are few things better than rewards for a job well done to motivate people to continue their hard work. The institution that places faculty rewards among its most important budgetary priorities will have a highly motivated faculty that will continue to perform in an outstanding way. A reward system also is essential to effective evaluation. When those who receive good evaluations also receive rewards, the evaluation system gains legitimacy. In addition, money rewards and motivation can be provided by ensuring that people receive credit for their activities and stand out among their peers. When other members of the leadership team receive compliments, the CAO looks even better. The CAO should give members of the leadership team due credit for their accomplishments so that the faculty will appreciate their efforts and understand their positions of responsibility.

Steps to Academic Change in the Participation Model

Achieving particular curricular and academic changes can be the most difficult task undertaken by the CAO. In most institutions the faculty must vote formal approval of the changes, but even in an institution where the change can be made without a faculty vote, faculty approval still is needed if the change is to be implemented successfully. If the five leadership principles discussed here are followed, the groundwork will have been laid for accomplishing specific changes, and then following the next six steps can help turn the academic leader's visions into realities.

1. Initiative. It has been said that the leader of any organization is the person with the initiative. While the debate in some institutions seems to be over who has authority, what matters is who has the initiative. The academic leader who has followed the five principles described earlier most likely will be able to take the initative in the first steps toward academic change. Listening to what is going on in the institution, taking leadership in articulating the institution's academic mission, and being aided by a leadership team should all foster initiative.

2. Problem Identification. Perhaps the most important step in bringing about academic change is achieving agreement on the existence and definition of a problem that needs to be solved. It is important that the academic leadership take the initiative in bringing the problem to the attention of the academic community and striving for consensus on problem definition. Facts and data, not hunches, must be used in setting forth the problem. The leadership should use a variety of forums and methods for discussing the problem until a consensus has been reached on its existence and the need for finding solutions. In the problem-identification stage it seems best to start small, to begin incrementally. It may be best to refrain from trying to convince others that the entire curriculum needs revision or that a complete faculty reorganization is desirable. A more politic approach may be first to identify smaller parts of problems and then allow solutions to several smaller problems add up to total curriculum revision. Once the problem has been identified, the leadership is ready to proceed to solutions.

3. *Broad Participation in Finding Solutions.* It is important to achieve consensus on problem identification before moving on to the solution stage because 90 percent of the time reasonable people will develop practically the same solution to a given problem. Consequently, once consensus on the problem has been reached, the leadership can decentralize the process of solving the problem and encourage the broadest possible involvement. Even in the 10 percent of cases in which a solution different from the leadership's is found, it probably will make little difference; a 90 percent success rate is not bad. Besides, broad participation in finding the solution is necessary to approval of the change and to its successful implementation, and opportunities for revising the solution will appear later.

Organization for broad participation will vary with circumstances. In a recent case at Birmingham–Southern we asked for task force volunteers to develop an introductory course for freshmen to solve long-standing problems with advising and orientation. A third of the faculty volunteered to serve. Because of this size, the task force was divided into four subcommittees. Also because there were so many people involved, all faculty members were kept informed of proceedings and were able to give advice and suggestions during the deliberations. In another case a faculty committee under the direction of an academic council member proposed a solution to a long-standing and agreed-on problem with the academic calendar for evening classes. Because the existence of the problem was so widely accepted, the faculty adopted the proposed solution unanimously. The irony of these two examples is that, in both cases, almost exactly the same solutions were the source of much campus controversy several years before when they were proposed for adoption without going through the problem-identification stage. During a faculty discussion of one of the proposals, a faculty member said, "If it ain't broke, don't fix it." The leadership had failed to establish that "it" was "broke." But the next time, when the process was followed, widespread agreement resulted.

4. *Acceptance of the Solution.* Once the leadership has invited broad participation in the process of finding a solution, it will have to

accept the solution that is proposed. Even though this point may sound somewhat frightening, it really is all right. In the great majority of cases — 90 percent — the solution found will be the one the leadership would have chosen. In the small number of cases in which a different solution is found, it probably will work anyway. Even if it does not work, the future will offer opportunities for revision. It would be a mistake for the leadership not to accept the faculty's solution, because the leadership's denial of its own process would ensure faculty refusal to accept leadership-initiated alternatives.

5. Delegation of Details. When it comes to curriculum changes and the adoption of new academic programs, the faculty must work in the programs and make them successful. Therefore, success seems most likely if those who work in a program have the primary responsibility for developing the implementation details. Moreover, it simply is not possible for the CAO to have a direct hand in the daily operation of everything, even new programs. The CAO's most important personal role does not come until later, in the evaluation and accountability phase. A very key role of the academic leadership in the process of planning implementation is to provide the necessary training and support for those who will be involved directly in program implementation. We should not assume that new programs can be started without advance preparation. The CAO should be assured that resources will be available for planning and preparation before the process of new program development begins. Just as the leadership team must be supported in performing its delegated responsibilities in its own way, so, too, must those who are implementing the details of new programs be supported. The member of the leadership team to whom people implementing the new program report will work closely with them to ensure overall leadership and responsibility.

6. Evaluation. The evaluation step is important because it is not only the process in which the change is held accountable to expectations, but also the process through which alterations can be made. The new program should be evaluated against the goals and objectives that were set for it. If the evaluation process identifies problems with the new program, the opportunity will be presented to begin the change process once again with initiative and problem identification. In a sense, then, these six steps for academic change form a cyclical process that begins anew with the evaluation step. Evaluation is the key both to accountability of implemented solutions and to solving new problems that arise. Because of responsibility for the evaluation process, the

CAO can continue to have the initiative and thereby maintain leadership.

Some may be concerned that this process of curriculum and academic program change poses too great a danger: Can the leadership or the CAO lose control of the process, with the result that changes take place in opposition to the leadership's goals? If the proper process is followed, there will be no loss of control. A far greater probability of failure exists when the leadership attempts to dictate change, because faculty displeasure will most likely cause failure of the implemented change.

The CAO plays two key roles in the change process, one at the beginning and the other at the end. The first key role is at the initiation and problem-identification stage. Successful identification of the problem to be solved will influence the solution that is proposed. The second key role is at the evaluation and accountability stage. The CAO's role here is to determine how well the change is working and, if necessary, initiate the change or problem-solving process anew. Performing these two roles successfully will ensure the CAO's leadership role. Most important, following all six steps of the change process will ensure that the change will be approved and accepted by the faculty and that its implementation will be successful.

Not everything the CAO does falls within the category of solving problems or initiating specific program changes. Consequently, this change process does not apply to all circumstances. It is useful, however, when the leadership has a particular change or program in mind or when a problem with the academic program surfaces and must be dealt with. In either case, it is important for the leadership of the academic program to maintain the initiative, and this process provides a means for doing so.

Conclusions

Peters and Waterman (1982) conclude their work on leadership in American business with what they call the *loose-tight* principle. They use this principle to serve as a summary point of their argument, and even though it was intended to apply to business leadership, it also serves as a good summary of the participation model. The essence of the participation model of academic leadership might be described in Peters and Waterman's words, as "the coexistence of firm central direction and maximum individual autonomy — what we call having one's cake and eating it too."

Firm central direction and maximum individual autonomy are really not incompatible concepts. The combination of the two, in fact, amounts to nothing more than President Truman's power to persuade people to do what they ought to have sense enough to do without being persuaded; it is exercising leadership by helping others participate in determining their own destiny. This model of leadership can be successful. The success comes, to quote Peters and Waterman (1982) again, "from treating people decently and asking them to shine." This is also the same point that has formed the basis of American political philosophy since 1776: The successful government is one that enjoys the consent of the governed.

Finally, the academic dean must accept leadership responsibility and recognize that leadership strategy is worth thinking about. How we do things is as important as what we do, simply because if we fail to do things by the right process, we will fail to get them done. The most difficult part of following these strategies for leadership may be having the patience to let the process work. Many academic leaders believe they already know what needs to be done, and many of them are right, but unless the faculty accepts the proposals, they will not be successful. Following the proper procedures presents the most likely probability of acceptance.

Thought Starters

1. Does the institution have a clearly understood, driving academic mission? Does the CAO articulate this mission on a regular basis?
2. Does the CAO have a leadership team? Are support and trust mutual between the team and the CAO?
3. Is there systematic and comprehensive evaluation within the academic program?
4. Is the campus infused with new ideas?
5. Is the CAO willing to have broad participation in the search for solutions to problems?

References

Neustadt, R. *Presidential Power.* New York: Wiley, 1958.

Peters, T., and Waterman, R. H., Jr. *In Search of Excellence: Lessons from America's Best-Run Companies.* New York: Harper and Row, 1982.

W. Edmund Moomaw is academic vice-president and dean of Birmingham-Southern College.

*The highly successful Career Redirection Program of
Regis College is described and placed in the context of
a multiple-option faculty development program, with its
accompanying theoretical rationale.*

Strategies for Faculty Development

William J. Hynes

February can rival April in the dean's calendar as the cruelest month.
Confronted with the rigidity and morbidity of the current system, even
the most optimistic in our ranks could find despair appropriate. February is the time of rank and tenure, impending contracts, and a pov-
erty of options. Objective scholars of sound judgment testify that normally fallible colleagues are now observed to walk on water. One has
the sinking feeling, that, lacking attractive alternatives, accidental academic liaisons are about to become permanent marriages.

This February is different. A sense of telos and inward compass
is abroad in the land. On my desk, four poignant requests have come to
rest. A full professor of business administration with twenty-six years of
teaching is asking to begin a gradual retirement program. His teaching
duties, faculty obligations, salary, and benefits will all be reduced by
half. He remarks that he wants to begin his retirement while he is "still
young and not bitter." A senior librarian has withdrawn her name from
consideration for the directorship of the library and has asked to be
considered for entrance into our career redirection program. This will
allow her a year, with full salary and benefits, to retrain for another
position outside of academe. She has a tremendously renewed sense of
enthusiasm and energy. A third proposal is from a senior Jesuit faculty

D. G. Brown (Ed.). *Leadership Roles of Chief Academic Officers.* New Directions
for Higher Education, no. 47. San Francisco: Jossey-Bass, September 1984.

member whose classes in recent years have been increasingly under-subscribed. He proposes a gradual retirement program which will ratchet his load down over four years until he is fully retired. He is clearly taking control of his life. A fourth proposal is from an academic administrator with faculty tenure requesting a year's leave of absence to explore a new career in personnel services. Several months into her leave, she will very likely take a new position. If this happens, she asks for the option of converting her leave into the career redirection program. She would then yield tenure and receive for three years a monthly payment from the college which would cover any negative differential between her new salary and the one she would have received at the college.

These proposals are but a few positive fruits of an overall plan for faculty development. Similar results are occurring in such parallel areas as teaching improvement, sabbaticals, research, professional activities, and the faculty handbook. The existence of a faculty development plan is essential for the intellectual vibrancy of a college or university. Another important benefit of such a program is that it can dramatically lighten the load shouldered by the dean.

The purpose of any such plan is to establish an attractive array of opportunities within faculty are encouraged toward continual professional development. What follows here is an attempt to set forth principles and strategies whereby one can encourage a high level of faculty development.

Principles for Faculty Development

Principle 1: Faculty Development Is a Continuous Process. This proposition may seem somewhat self-evident. The purpose of a faculty development plan is to establish opportunities that encourage faculty to pursue continual professional growth rather than stagnation. It is crucial to establish the principle that even the best of teachers always has something more to learn; even the best researcher has another technique or area of study to be pursued. A faculty development plan is counterposed to the constant temptation of simply resting on one's laurels, however modest these may be. Faculty development or improvement is rather more like John Steinbeck's comment on the Holy Grail: "It is not an object, but a promise which skips ahead ever beyond our grasp." Faculty development should be a continuous process leading us ever beyond today's accomplishments.

By the same token, a faculty development plan can be a source a strength and patience for a new dean. What is needed in all such situations is a clear and consistent statement about what constitutes a good faculty member and the certainty that all aspects of the system support it. In such new situations, there are undoubtedly some solid faculty members, perhaps overlooked by the dean, who basically need to be encouraged so that they will flourish and have a good chance of becoming the leaven in the mass. At the other extreme, there are faculty who will need to be replaced. In the middle are many faculty who may have potential, if properly encouraged, to become solid contributors. Before you decide to replace this group with imported talent, which can also bring its own imported problems, consider trying to "grow your own." This is not to imply that the dean is the master gardener and the faculty the garden; the growth must be self-chosen and self-directed by the faculty.

Principle 2: The Initiative for Faculty Development Should Come Primarily from Faculty. A natural place from which such a plan can emanate is a faculty development committee. After the plan evolves and is reviewed and approved by all concerned parties, it should be reflected in an accessible constitutive document, such as a faculty handbook.

A program to improve the teaching process, for example, can consist of such things as workshops on specific teaching techniques (group processes, Socratic method, audiovisual uses, computer simulations). Small grants for this purpose can be made available and allocated by a faculty committee. One of the most successful techniques is to combine several competitive grants with a mandatory workshop. Thus, several faculty members might receive $1,500–3,000 during the summer to redesign existing courses. Part of the requirement for such grants would be attendance at a one-week workshop devoted to teaching techniques.

Although there are parallel actions a dean can take to strengthen the development process, it is a good idea in general to let the initial and greatest impetus behind faculty development be the faculty development committee itself. To have faculty development seen as being pushed or required by the administration can be the kiss of death.

Principle 3: Seed Money Versus the Money Trap. You can have a faculty development plan with or without new or massive sums of money. In certain ways, money does facilitate the process: It is obviously helpful if modest amounts of seed money can be allocated to pro-

vide honoraria to faculty for course redesign work or stipends for summer research or professional faculty travel. At the same time, this plan
can turn into a medieval fee or piecework system, in which a faculty
member has been conditioned not to pursue such activities unless there
is a specific monetary reward. There is nothing like a grant proposal to
help invent a plan or extend a modest effort into something larger or
more permanent. Indeed, this is how many faculty development programs came into existence. A Lilly Endowment grant of $90,000 allowed
Regis College to start its faculty development program a decade ago.
Fairleigh Dickinson University began its program on three campuses
several years ago after receiving a grant of $200,000 from a local foun-
dation. It should be noted, however, that there is generally less funding
available today for faculty development.

Faculty development includes a wide range of activities. At
Regis we begin each academic year with a fall faculty conference. This
starts, typically, with an academic convocation on Friday honoring our
teacher of the year, who delivers a major address. The following Satur-
day the faculty convenes for an all-day conference or workshop. In
recent years these have included such topics as "The Liberal Arts: Pure
or Applied," "Application of Personality Typologies to Teaching and
Team Building," "Computer Applications for the Classroom," and
"Integrating New Research on Women into the Curriculum." During
the year there is a wide variety of activities, including a series of brown-
bag lunches featuring home faculty and administrators, guest speakers,
a readers' theater, opportunities for faculty to report on their research
and sabbatical activities, and workshops on developing skills for such
things as consulting and interviewing. Given this level of activity, it
does help if there is at least a part-time secretary to support and coordi-
nate faculty development.

*Principle 4: Distinguish Teaching Improvement from Teaching
Effectiveness.* It is important to distinguish between activities aimed
at improving teaching and the formal demonstration of teaching effectiveness. At base simply an attempt not to confuse input with output,
this differentiation has several advantages. First, it respects the principle stated earlier: that teaching improvement should ideally be self-
generated. Second, it separates learning from the evaluation of actual
teaching. Finally, it protects everyone from the erroneous conclusion
that activity in the first area automatically is equated with success in
the second. It is advisable to incorporate such a distinction into the formal criteria for promotion in rank or to tenure.

The distinction between teaching improvement and teaching effectiveness parallels the distinction between summative and process evaluation. The latter occurs at the end of a process, when nothing can be undone, and is generally a judgment of someone as good or bad. Process evaluation takes place while things can still change and does not result in judgment about the person. Process evaluation is primarily of benefit to those actually engaged in the particular process. Summative evaluation is more appropriate at the time of rank and tenure actions.

Strategies for the Chief Academic Officer or Dean

In general, the academic administrator in this area should set the general context of expectations for faculty development while leaving many of the specifics to the faculty, particularly the faculty development committee.

Strategy 1: Cycles of Success and Rituals of Reward. Appearances to the contrary, it is sometimes useful to treat academe as if it were a system. It is good to examine the system and assess whether it really does reward the behavior we say is important. If we say that we are a teaching institution, is it our best teachers who receive tenure and promotion? If we say that we value academic excellence, where do we celebrate its achievement? If we demand research from our faculty, do we support this activity?

We need to take a given attainment of excellence and trace it through the system to ensure that it is being acknowledged and celebrated in all possible ways. For example, our Regis Teacher of the Year awards ceremony is an event open to the entire college community, although specific groups receive printed invitations: faculty, administration and appropriate staff, students on the dean's list, students on academic or leadership scholarships, the board of trustees, the family of the honored faculty member, and anyone else the honoree wishes to invite. Following a lecture, there is a lunch. The lecture is often covered by the local press. For the past two years, we have printed the lecture in an attractive format and circulated this to a wider audience.

Strategy 2: Procedures for Promotion in Rank and to Tenure. A dean can attempt to ensure that the pertinent criteria and evidence required for any application for advancement in rank and to tenure will adequately reflect the need for professional growth. You do well to specify not only the criteria but the type of evidence that might be submitted. This could include evidence of activities undertaken to improve knowledge of one's field, use of additional teaching techniques, professional work, research, and publications.

Strategy 3: Enlistment of the Departmental Chairs. In meeting with department chairs and reviewing progress toward annual goals, the dean can regularly inquire into the progress of faculty members of each department toward professional growth. Such inquiry can serve to encourage the department chair to monitor such information. Academics are often Edwardian enough to assume that it is bad form to inquire into the professional well-being of a colleague. Such inquiry is always timely, particularly for junior colleagues, who should be making solid progress toward fulfilling the requirements for promotion in rank and to tenure.

Strategy 4: Midcareer or Career Redirection Programs. Redirection programs allow faculty to choose new careers while diminishing normal financial and status impediments to career change. The Regis Career Redirection Program is formally restricted to tenured faculty who have ten or more years of service to the college. It is initiated by the faculty member concerned and must be approved by the administration.

There are two options within the plan. First, a faculty member may ask to be relieved from all campus duties for one year so that he or she can pursue retraining or the establishment of an individual firm. During this period, faculty receive their normal salaries and retain their academic titles, and they agree to yield their academic tenure and not to accept a new position within the field of education. At the end of the year, the title of Professor Emeritus/a and $3,000 career redirection grant are awarded. In addition, a number of modest privileges normally associated with retirement also continue. Costs are easily amortized over several years, particularly when it is understood that—generally in the first year, when the full salary is being paid—the departing person will be replaced by a part-time faculty member. In the second year, when a full-time replacement is sought, the position is generally filled by someone at a junior level and a lesser salary. The second option is for faculty members who do not need a period for retraining or for establishing independent income. One impediment, however, could be a possible negative differential between the academic salary and the new income. The college will make up any negative differential on a monthly basis for three years, provided that the new salary is more than $12,000.

An academic institution that begins such a program must realize that the administration cannot control who chooses it. This must be a program available to all. Furthermore, you must be prepared for the possibility that some of your best faculty will enter it. So be it. What is important is the liberating and enfranchising atmosphere associated with increasing the range of options available to an increasingly immobile faculty. Faculty have a major new career option. Observing individuals who have pursued this program at Regis, I have been struck by the new levels of energy, creativity, and enthusiasm in the lives of these individuals.

Strategy 5: Graduated Retirement. A graduated or phased retirement program simply allows faculty members to enter retirement in stages. Generally, this means that in a given year, they could request to have their teaching load reduced by a small amount, say one quarter. They retain prorated tenure and can continue to wind down their teaching in similar increments until full retirement is achieved. It is a good idea to have health and life insurance benefits continue in full force until full retirement. Pension contributions by the college are adjusted as the amount of compensation diminishes.

It is also a good idea to include two additional provisions in such a plan. First, you may wish to include a ratchet clause, so that a faculty member whose duties have decreased to a certain level is not able to reverse the phaseout. Second, the faculty member initiates the plan and at any time can hold to wherever point is already reached. Thus, a person working half-time can stay at this point until mandatory retirement.

Strategy 6: Early Retirement Plan. One program of this type offers a one-time stipend equal to 100 percent of full salary to faculty who retire at age sixty-two. The amount available decreases by at least 10 percent per year, until there is no more economic incentive for early retirement. This occurs at age seventy, when retirement is mandatory.

Strategy 7: Interinstitutional Agreements. No institution ever has all the resources it needs. If we overcome our sense of private domain, any number of arrangements can be made to share resources. These arrangements can include one-way or two-way faculty exchanges between similar institutions. Today corporations often have library and electronic resources far exceeding those available at colleges and universities. There are also opportunities for visiting and exchange fellows from the corporate sector, similar to the successful IBM program.

The foregoing principles and strategies are ways in which the

38

dean or the chief academic officer can encourage faculty to enter into a process of self-development. In all of this activity, it is crucial that the academic leadership speak in a unified and consistent voice. No one item must be utilized all the time, but acknowledged. On good days, synergy can develop: The total effect is greater than the sum of the individual parts. One person's discernible success and its acknowledgement can serve as a stimulus for others to go forth into their own areas of professional self-development and adventure.

Sources

Baldwin, R. G., Brakeman, L., Edgerton, R., Hagberg, J., and Maher, T. *Expanding Faculty Options: Career Development Projects at Colleges and Universities.* Washington, D.C.: American Association for Higher Education, 1981.

Baldwin, R. G., and Blackburn, R. T. (Eds.). *College Faculty: Versatile Human Resources in a Period of Contraint.* New Directions for Institutional Research, no. 40. San Francisco: Jossey-Bass, 1983.

Furniss, W. T. *Reshaping Faculty Careers.* Washington, D.C.: American Council on Education, 1981.

Furniss, W. T. *The Self-Reliant Academic.* Washington, D.C.: American Council on Education, 1984.

Hodgkinson, H. "Adult Development: Implications for Faculty and Administrators." *Educational Record,* 1974, *55* (4), 263-274.

Levinson, D. C., Darrow, C. N., Klein, E. G., Levinson, M. H., and McKee, B. *The Seasons of a Man's Life.* New York: Knopf, 1978.

Lightman, M., and Zeisel, M. (Eds.). *Outside Academe: New Ways of Working in the Humanities.* New York: Halworth Press, 1981.

McKeachie, W. J. "Older Faculty Members: Facts and Prescriptions." *AAHE Bulletin,* 1983, *36* (3), 8-10.

Patton, C. V. *Academia in Transition: Mid-Career Change or Early Retirement.* Cambridge, Mass.: Abbot Books, 1979.

Thoreson, R. W. "The Professor at Risk: Alcohol Abuse in Academe." *Journal of Higher Education,* 1984, *55* (1), 56-72.

William J. Hynes is dean of campus programs at Regis College.

No activities of the chief academic officer have more
important consequences than the hiring of new faculty
and the nurturing of faculty leadership.

Sustaining Faculty Leadership

John Oppelt

The chief academic officer should have vision, creativity, and the courage to demand flexibility in all programs. This flexibility comes mostly from the type of faculty who are hired (and chances have to be taken), from the atmosphere created for existing faculty, from encouragement for the university's faculty to grow, and from a faculty/administrative structure that is intelligently founded on the mission of the college and results in mutual rewards for those delivering the institution's message (the faculty) and those primarily responsible for making it coherent (the administration).

Successful recruitment starts with defining the position for which you are recruiting. For example, if you want leadership in the school of business because you are seeking accreditation, then you should look for a person with experience and familiarity with accreditation standards. If you are trying to build a data processing program that would have ties to the community, it may be wise to recruit someone already in the business world, not a computer scientist from an academic institution. Even more important are candidates' personal characteristics, such as ability to be entrepreneurial, articulate, and imaginative. You should not hire for special trends; instead, hire faculty who indicate that they are now and will continue to be not only good in their fields but also able to reach out, expand, and grow.

D. G. Brown (Ed.). *Leadership Roles of Chief Academic Officers.* New Directions for Higher Education, no. 47. San Francisco: Jossey-Bass, September 1984.

Risks must be taken by everyone participating in the search. Consideration of the individual candidate should predominate. To decide whether the match between candidate and position is right, communicate the institutional mission clearly and incisively and assure the candidate that he or she will have a say in the future of the program. Having found a good candidate, you should be fairly persistent. The pursuit usually will involve others: A potential member of the accounting faculty may be swayed by the attentions of the dean of the school of business, a key faculty member, or prominent members of the business community.

You should also present your institution's limitations honestly. Good communication requires not only information about positive factors (growing endowment, special projects under way) but also an explanation of present or potential difficulties (declining salary increments, interpersonal problems within the faculty). This gives the recruit a clear sense of belonging to the community and diminishes later surprises.

Once hired, a faculty member must be nurtured to share the vision of where the institution is heading, what his or her changing role may be, and how he or she may be assisted in attaining the prerequisite skills for the role. Nurturance demands constant and clear communication of goals as well as priorities that go beyond the setting of curricula, the initial hiring of faculty, and the reward system of merit and promotion. Typically, the institution recognizes this responsibility for nurturance in the form of sabbaticals, visiting professors, colloquiums, funds for travel to professional meetings, reduced teaching loads, leaves of absence, and library support. All these devices are important for continued faculty development, but too often they are used without purpose. Granted, if you want mathematicians to be better at what they do, you must give them the time to be creative and the associations to allow their creativity to expand. In contrast, if you want topologists to contribute to a new operations research program in the mathematics department, then they should know where you are heading and why, should have enough information to participate, should be flexible enough to want to, and should be encouraged by specific awards. These include a sabbatical to expand from topology into modern applied mathematics, exposure to colloquia offered by experts in operations research and supported by the institution, or reduced teaching loads and tuition support to expand expertise. Sometimes nurturance may mean hiring persons credentialed at the master's level, with the explicit purpose of supporting them through reduced teaching loads and in-house fellowships so that they can earn the doctorate.

Always keep in mind, too, the tenured faculty member or the long-term academic administrator who has given much to the institution and the profession, but who has become somewhat dormant and unimaginative. This is a time for risk taking. Grant a sabbatical or a reduced teaching load to such an individual, and the spark may fire; it often does. I believe the institution is indebted in many cases; it can only be rewarded as a result of risk taking.

Tenure

Those responsible for a tenure decision ideally should envision the long-term future of the faculty member, present needs and future of the department and the college, how fields and programs may change, the long-term makeup of the faculty, needs of future leaders within the institution, and the institution's relationship to its external constituencies. In reality, though, tenure decisions seem to be made on the basis of other considerations: Is this person a prolific publisher? Is this person reasonably good in the classroom? (There is seldom any evaluation). Does this person have a reasonably good personality? (If the individual is a successful researcher, the probability of a good personality is diminished.)

If we accept the ideal elements of decisions regarding tenure, promotion, or merit increases, then such decisions are really about the growth, flexibility, developing leadership, and continuing creativity of the candidate. Tenure decisions, for example, should encourage individuals to contribute to the department and college goals. But, given the actual tenure process, decisions about the future of the institution are in fact often made when a faculty member is invited to join the college. Hence, the importance of the search process becomes predominant, because you need to choose individuals capable of the flexibility, creativity, and growth the institution requires in its full professors.

Thoughts Regarding the Curriculum

Curriculum development is an elite activity. To different degrees, that is true in the smallest liberal arts colleges as well as in the largest state universities. Choose an upper-level course, and you will find it taught by one person, even if other experts exist. Look at general

education requirements, and you will know the most powerful departments in the institution. Look at what constitutes a major, and you will
know the fields of the more influential or better-entrenched professors.

Curriculum planning is complex because it must simultaneously
maintain three ideals: true values, living in the present, and looking to
the future. The first value can elicit excesses of expertise, the second can
cause trendiness, and the third is at best chancy and can lead one down
the wrong path.

If faculty are aware of financial constraints, are allowed to take
some risks in curriculum development (with the possibility of changes),
develop the curriculum to be flexible (keeping the nontraditional student
in mind), and are rewarded for their work, then a lively intellectual environment will result.

*John Oppelt is vice-president for academic affairs
at Bellarmine College.*

Reallocation of positive reductions in staffing and urgent retrenchments will require a consistently open process.

The Process of Academic Governance and the Painful Choices of the 1980s

Kenneth P. Mortimer
Annette C. Caruso

Three probable institutional needs can be forecast from data and trends available in 1984: the need to reallocate people and programs in response to changing student demand, the need for some institutions to get smaller, and the need for short-term retrenchment. Approximately 60 to 65 percent of baccalaureate degrees now awarded by American four-year colleges and universities are in preprofessional education. This is exactly the reverse of the situation in the early 1970s. Institutions have found it very difficult to reallocate faculty resources to deal with shifting student interest patterns.

There is anecdotal evidence that need to reallocate internal resources exacerbates existing tensions among faculty and administrators in various areas of the campus. For example, in spite of an almost doubling of the student credit hours generated in the College of Business at the University of Colorado, when the administration proposed that no cuts be made in the College of Business faculty, the powerful lobby

D. G. Brown (Ed.). *Leadership Roles of Chief Academic Officers.* New Directions for Higher Education, no. 47. San Francisco: Jossey-Bass, September 1984.

bloc of the College of Arts and Sciences insisted that any cuts be made proportionately among all the colleges, regardless of faculty teaching loads.

Seventy-nine percent of the chief academic officers in four-year colleges and universities who respond to the Project on Reallocation survey reported that they were engaged in significant reallocations within their areas of resonsibility. The CAOs were also experimenting with several devices to try to control the amount of reallocation necessary. For example, 31 percent of the institutions had enrollment caps of some sort, 84 percent of the institutions reported that the campus administration had final say over whether to fill a faculty vacancy, and approximately 28 percent of the institutions had tenure quotas.

Reduction in Size. Some institutions will find it necessary to reduce the size of their faculties in the coming years. For example, an analysis of Montana State University's potential showed ". . . that MSU will, over the next ten years, face reductions in the size of the faculty greater than the number of· openings created by retirement. Because the national job market may also be very bleak, it was further assumed that faculty members will attempt to remain in their present jobs for as long as possible. The extreme version of this assumption, that no resignations will be submitted except for retirement, projects a very bleak picture in which perhaps an average of twelve faculty members per year will have to be involuntarily terminated. Further, if tenure is granted to 90 percent of those currently on track, the entire faculty could conceivably be tenured" (Otzenberger and Kaelke, 1980, p. 5).

Johnstone (1980) reports that the staffing ratio at Montana State University went from 14:1 in 1960 to 19:1 in 1979, and he implies that it has reached its limit. Minter and Bowen's (1982) national surveys report only a slight change in the ratio of faculty members to students: Full-time equivalents were about 14.7:1 in 1969–1970 and 14.1:1 in 1979–1980. We found numerous cases where student–faculty ratios became the focus of fiscal control, too. Hruby (1973) suggests that these ratios were part of Aquinas College's struggle for financial stability.

There are only three basic ways to increase the student–faculty ratio: to increase the number of students and hold the number of faculty constant, reduce the number of faculty and hold the number of students constant, or develop some combination of the two approaches. These three approaches have distinctly different income and expenditure implications. In an era of declining resources, specifically in terms of enrollments, many institutions will find it necessary to reduce faculty just to maintain established student–faculty ratio policies.

Retrenchment. The need for short-term faculty layoffs or dismissals may well be more common in the 1980s than it was in the 1970s. Arguments over such retrenchment conditions tend to revolve around what constitutes bona fide financial emergency and program discontinuance. Approximately 39 percent of our respondents to the Project on Reallocation had financial exigency statements in 1981, but only 8 percent had used them since 1977. In addition, 34 percent had written retrenchment policies.

From our data, we are able to estimate that approximately 4,000 faculty members in four-year colleges and universities were dismissed or laid off in the period 1977–1982. Almost all dismissals and layoffs were in the so-called invisible and comprehensive colleges, and about 1,250 of these faculty members were tenured.

Characteristics of Academic Decision Making

As this chapter is being written, the national higher education community is in the midst of a love affair with strategic planning. The implication of this movement is that administrators will need to set priorities to aid in making difficult choices associated with the decision contexts identified above. The assumption seems to be that contexts of reallocation, reduction, and retrenchment will require making forced choices among desirable alternatives. A forced-choice decision-making environment will focus greater attention on such matters as the legitimacy and trustworthiness of the decision-making process as well as of the criteria used to arrive at difficult judgments about terminations, program closures, and reductions.

The legitimacy of academic governance is based on mutual trust and cooperation among participants. Planning is essential, but the need for legitimacy in governance puts increased emphasis on the question of who can be trusted to make final decisions. If the tone of faculty-administration relations is adversarial and characterized by a conflict-of-interst mentality, then the free information so crucial to effective decision making and planning will not be available to all parties. For example, when relations are highly adversarial, control of information may become a political tool to be used according to the political advantage it affords.

To maintain essential patterns of legitimacy and trust, institutions' approach to governance in the late 1980s and the 1990s should be characterized by a high degree of openness — open plans, open policy statements, open rules, open findings, open reasons, open precedents, and fair informal and formal procedures. The reason for repeating the word *open* is a powerful one: openness is the natural enemy of arbitrariness and the natural ally of the struggle for trust and legitimacy.

We believe there are five elements that will be important in establishing or maintaining a high degree of openness and trust as colleges and universities seek to make difficult decisions in the late 1980s and the early 1990s:

1. Early consultation: Participants in a problem-solving process must have a chance to consider the formulation of alternatives as well as the phrasing of issues before the alternatives become rigidified.

2. Joint formulation of procedures: An agreement over the appropriate process to be followed is a vital part of relationships built on trust and joint endeavor.

3. Time to formulate responses: A common source of irritation for participants in college and university governance is the request for advice that has to be rendered immediately. While many such requests are legitimate — time is short — too often they merely reflect sloppy planning or inadequate anticipation of problems.

4. Availability of information: Those who would restrict the free flow of information in academic affairs should be prepared to justify that restriction. The budgets of public institutions are often public documents, and the only remaining question is how much detail to make available.

5. Adequate feedback: A basic principle of consultation should be that when a decision is made, it is communicated both to the people who rendered the advice and counsel and to the community at large.

We are optimistic that faculty committees operating in open atmospheres of trust and legitimacy will be effective participants in the difficult judgments concerning academic vitality, and even cuts in the 1990s. It has been suggested elsewhere that faculty committees work best when they are asked about procedures, methods, and criteria for arriving at judgments, rather than about making decisions on which programs should be discontinued or which faculty members should be laid off. We continue to believe the effectiveness of such decisions will be substanially influenced by the degree of openness and trust prevalent on the campus.

References

Hruby, N. J. *A Survival Kit for Invisible Colleges: What to Do Until Federal Aid Arrives.* Washington, D.C.: Management Division, Academy for Educational Development, 1973.

Johnstone, W. A. "Faculty Retrenchment in the 1980's: A Question of How Many? and How Managed?" *The Journal of the College and University Personnel Association,* 1980, *31,* 22–30.

Minter, J. W., and Bowen, H. R. "Despite Economic Ills, Colleges Weathered the 60's with Larger Enrollments and Stronger Programs." *Chronicle of Higher Education,* 1982, 5–7.

Otzenberger, S. J., and Kaelke, M. E. "The MSU Scenario: A Basis for Discussion." *The Journal of the College and University Personnel Association,* 1980, *31,* 1–6.

Kenneth P. Mortimer and Annette C. Caruso are both leaders of the Project on Reallocation. They are associated with the Center for the Study of Higher Education at Pennsylvania State University.

If properly handled, reallocation can provide a rich
opportunity for enhancing quality, but there is no easy
way to reallocate resources.

Using the Instructional Budget
to Maintain Quality

Christine A. Young

Members of college and university faculties and academic administrators
face two potentially conflicting imperatives in this decade: the enhancement of academic quality and reduction of instructional expenses. The
management of decline runs counter to the collegial governance of
higher education and against the grain of American culture, which has
always celebrated growth and expansion. Deans who do not argue for
larger budgets may be accused by their faculties of "treasonable or irre-
sponsible leadership," and in some cases those who must cut budgets
become objects of efforts to "destroy leaders by investigative reporting,
unwarranted criticisms, and character assassination" (Powers, 1982,
pp. 9–10). Howard Bowen (1982, p. 10) has noted, "Many presidents
and deans who have dared to propose specific budget cuts are under
siege. The magnitude of the problem varies among institutions but few
are totally exempt. It is not a happy time in academe."

Decreasing Expenditures

The operating budgets of most colleges approximate 25 percent
for faculty, 14 percent for staffing, 18 percent for general service

D. G. Brown (Ed.). *Leadership Roles of Chief Academic Officers.* New Directions
for Higher Education, no. 47. San Francisco: Jossey-Bass, September 1984.

workers, and 43 percent for nonpersonnel expenditures (Bowen, 1982). All cost centers need to be involved in the search for savings, with the proportion to be borne by each determined by the particular circumstances of the institution. For example, if a decline in numbers of students (and their tuition dollars) is the primary reason for the quest for savings, then it would stand to reason that fewer faculty are needed and that other expenses related directly to enrollment (for example, financial aid) might also be reduced, but not that library expenditures should be reduced (unless programs are cut).

"The search for savings should not overlook such items as general administration, plant maintenance, capital expenditures, fuel and utilities" (Bowen, 1982, p. 10). Similarly, the search for additional revenues should involve all sectors. Ginsburg (1982) has provided checklists of ways to increase revenues and decrease expenditures. Ginsburg's checklists illustrate both points: Only six of the thirty-five ideas for increasing income involve academic programs, while fifteen of the eighty-five ideas for decreasing expenses concern faculty and academic programs.

Means of reducing instructional expenditures identified by Ginsburg (1982), Mingle and Norris (1981), and Meeth (1974) include the following for programs:

1. Reduce the number of courses and course sections.
2. Reduce course duplication in different colleges or departments.
3. Phase out or eliminate majors, programs, and so forth that are not centrally important to the institutional mission, of high quality, and available at low cost, if the institution is also unlikely to be able to raise quality or offset costs.
4. Reduce costs or add teaching time by combining programs or departments.
5. Reduce costs by using new instructional technologies.
6. Limit the number of electives for each major.
7. Establish minimum class sizes.
8. Schedule low-enrollment classes only for alternate years.
9. Establish goals for the faculty–student ratio, and use the best combination of strategies to meet ratio goals.

Several of these suggestions constitute economic guidelines for the curriculum (limits on the number of electives, minimum class sizes, alternate-year scheduling) and, depending on how many of these guidelines are already in place, could result in substantial savings without reducing quality or the total number of programs and majors in an institution. For example, Meeth (1974, p. 171) urges small colleges to offer "no more than six to twelve hours beyond the number required for the major in any academic year," while Bowen and Douglass (1972, pp. 33–34) advise "no more than eleven different courses per year in a subject, or 225 different courses for a total institution." Bowen boldly asserts, "On the testimony of experienced and capable teachers, the number of courses offered in a typical undergraduate college could be halved without harming educational quality." With equal boldness, Meeth (1974, p. 172) suggests that "if public institutions can produce a reasonably qualified graduate at [a faculty–student ratio of 1:19 or 1:20]... there is no reason to believe that private institutions cannot do as well."

Given the greater difficulty of choosing which programs to eliminate or combine, consideration of such guidelines by faculty and academic administrators is the best first step for colleges and universities. Implementation of these guidelines does not, however, satisfy the need to review each program to ensure consistency with the mission of the institution and its standards of quality. Whether the purpose of such review is strengthening all programs or eliminating those of lower quality or importance to the institution, some combination of the two approaches — establishing economic guidelines for the curriculum and reviewing programs for quality and centrality — will probably be needed by most institutions.

Reshaping the curriculum, whether through streamlining of existing programs and majors or selective elimination of a few, will result in a decreased need for faculty. Reducing the size of a faculty is never easy; decisions must be tailored to the particular situation of each college or university. Options include the following:

1. Leave vacant positions unfilled (attrition).
2. Establish early retirement plans.
3. Move faculty into administrative vacancies.
4. Reclassify faculty vacancies as non–tenure track.
5. Tighten standards for tenure (Bowen, 1982).
6. Assign faculty, as qualified, to teach courses in other departments (for example, a philosopher to teach intellectual history) Mingle and Norris, 1981).
7. Retrain faculty through paid leaves or sabbaticals to teach courses in growing departments.
8. Terminate faculty appointments as a consequence of course or program discontinuance.

Selective use of these options is necessary; none will work well in all institutions.

To date, much attention has been focused on the last of these options, and not enough on the others. When an institution is required to reduce the instructional budget quickly, the strategies for reallocating faculty over a period of time (while taking advantage of retirements and resignations that occur in areas of declining need) will not suffice to avoid involuntary terminations. For example, Heydinger (1982) reports that in 1981, when the University of Minnesota was given two weeks to respond to a request for a retrenchment budget, the plan submitted had to include a number of faculty position eliminations. Even in this case, however, a number of "creative" retirements were arranged. Ongoing trend analysis and planning are the best protection against having to engage in involuntary terminations, but it is doubtful that the best long-range planning by the most clairvoyant administrators and faculty can completely eliminate the risk of retrenchment in this era of rapid demographic shifts and equally sudden changes in public support for higher education.

Choosing a Strategy for Reduction

Even after colleges and universities have implemented economic guidelines for the curriculum, reducing the number of courses accordingly, and have used all appropriate strategies short of retrenchment for reallocating and reducing faculty resources, some institutions will face the need to make additional reductions, often within a very short time. The choices available fall into two broad categories: across-the-board cuts and selective program (and faculty) elimination. In a cogent "debate" with Bowen, Newman (1982) outlined the relative merits of each approach.

Across-the-board cuts are generally perceived as fair and are consistent with the norms of collegiality. The structure of the organization is left intact, the tenure system is not undermined, and the governance system for deliberation about educational policy can proceed in its usual manner. Furthermore, there are precedents for two different kinds of across-the-board approaches: actual salary cuts (as during the Depression of the 1930s) and erosion of purchasing power of faculty and staff salaries (as during the 1970s and the 1980s, due to inflation) (Bowen, 1982). Bowen and Newman agree that a major disadvantage of across-the-board cuts is the inability to reallocate faculty resources to program areas of increasing demand, but their individual assessments of the institutional consequences of this static mode differ in important ways.

Bowen argues that institutions should not be at the mercy of the careerist motives of many students in the 1980s and should, indeed, attempt to redirect such motives as possible. Newman's assessment of the consequences of across-the-board cuts is quite negative. For the small number ("perhaps fifty") of elite institutions that are still generously funded, this method may be an appropriate holding action, he says, but most institutions have already suffered considerable erosion not only of educational quality but also of earning power of faculty salaries through inflation; they cannot expect relief through increased enrollments or external funding in the near future. For such institutions, which have effectively been diminished already through higher-than-average cost increases in key sectors of the budget (library, faculty travel, laboratory equipment), further decreases will result in "leaky roofs and demoralized faculty" (Newman, 1982). Academic quality in such institutions will suffer from continued erosion through inflation or deliberate across-the-board cuts. Newman also rejects the notion that higher education should be static, since it has such a long history of dynamic response to the changing needs of the societies it has served.

When Bowen and Newman consider the relative merits of selective program elimination, once again their views are both cogent and different.

The disadvantages of selective reduction, when laid out, are certainly enough to give an academic administrator pause. According to Bowen (1982, p. 12), the decisions will always appear to be unjust to at least a few faculty members, regardless of the process used; some faculty careers will be destroyed, and the administrators responsible will be placed in "a vulnerable position," while a general air of insecurity dominates the campus: "In short, selective retrenchment, if pushed very far, is likely to be highly damaging to organizational morale. And morale is a key to institutional effectiveness—especially in hard times." Recent research buttresses Bowen's contention that administrative careers, particularly those of chief academic officers responsible for program elimination, are short-lived. Newman (1982) agrees that selective program elimination is hard and frustrating, but argues that the integrity and, perhaps, the survival of higher education depend on pursuing quality at the expense (potential and perhaps temporary) of collegiality.

In reviewing the advantages of setting priorities and eliminating a few programs to augment resources available to the survivors, Bowen, an economist, agrees (1982) that this approach is "consistent with accepted economic reasoning" about allocating greater resources to areas of strength or high priority while eliminating or diminishing support for programs of lower priority. He argues, however, that in the case of higher education, rational allocation strategies may well work against institutional "effectiveness." Newman (1982) thinks, in contrast, that setting priorities among programs is the best way to "insure that there are incentives for quality and change, and that each university moves toward its own special character and mission."

These two positions, founded on rich experience and careful reflection, are equally worthy of discussion and study by those administrators and faculty members who must choose a retrenchment strategy for their institutions. In the end, Newman asserts that few institutions can afford across-the-board reductions because the quality of the educational enterprise will be severely (additionally) damaged, while Bowen urges reconsideration of across-the-board cuts because few institutions can afford the inevitable damage to morale following program elimination. Bowen (1982, p. 10) also advises that "there are many ways to retrench, that each institution should find the least destructive combination, and that restraint in the use of the selective approach is advisable."

Program Planning and Evaluation: The Criteria

Academic administrators and faculty leaders who choose some form of programmatic reduction will need to establish criteria for program elimination. Fortunately, several major universities and a number of smaller colleges have forged detailed statements of criteria for ranging programs in priority order, with the implicit or explicit purpose of dropping programs at the bottom. These statements, prepared in the face of a need to reduce budgets, are called retrenchment guidelines, but they are very similar to what are now standard guidelines for strategic planning that are recommended for institutions at all points along the spectrum of fiscal health. Standard entries include centrality, quality, demand, and cost.

Centrality. Centrality, or relevance to the institution's mission, will have particular meanings in different settings (Mingle and Norris, 1981; Powers, 1982). One institution may declare "a broad curriculum in the humanities, social sciences, and natural sciences" plus "high-quality professional schools" to be its "core" and thereby relegate all other programs to secondary status (Franklin, 1982, p. 35); another may rank each program according to the degree to which it incorporates and satisfies multiple purposes of the institution — teaching, research, and service (Heydinger, 1982). If a program does not have a high number of majors but serves elective needs of other programs, its "connectedness" must also be taken into account in determining centrality (Heydinger, 1982).

Quality. Like centrality, quality is a controversial term that may have many meanings. The quality of a program's structure and content may be measured by agreed-upon standards against other programs in the institution, against similar programs at other institutions (Powers, 1982) or against some ideal. Alternatively, an assessment of program quality may be "based on a consideration of the quality of the student body, when compared both with those of other universities... and the quality of the faculty" (Franklin, 1982, p. 35). Since the achievement of quality is "often the result of the happy combination of opportunity, good luck, and foresight" (Heydinger, 1982, p. 7), some institutions may decide to judge programs in terms of "potential quality over the next several years" (Mingle and Norris, 1981, p. 6). Assessments of quality will thus depend on whether an institution bases its standards on faculty, students, the programs themselves, or a mixture of the three, as well as on whether the assessment takes into account recent trends and probable futures.

Demand. Every institution includes the current demand for courses among its criteria for program planning, evaluation, and potential reduction. Enrollment trends and projections based on anticipated employment opportunities for graduates are also standard measures of program viability. Simple analyses of enrollments and job prospects, however, may lead to inappropriate conclusions about the demand for particular programs, especially if they serve important research or service functions (Heydinger, 1982), or enroll disproportionately growing or shrinking sectors of the student population.

Some institutions approach the question of program demand from yet another point of view: whether similar programs of equal or higher quality are available at lower cost within the geographic area. Franklin (1982, p. 35) says that "a great private university must be composed of educational components which are better than or different from those in public universities, if, in the long run, it will be able to

56

charge higher tuition and continue to achieve a high level of support from corporations, foundations, and individuals donors" and remain attractive to cost-conscious students and their parents. Conversely, a major public university lists "uniqueness" among its six criteria for program planning, meaning that a special mission, such as that of a land-grant university, may tip the balance toward retaining specialized programs that other colleges and universities do not incorporate within their missions (Heydinger, 1982).

Cost. Far from a simple accounting exercise, determining the cost of continuing or eliminating a program of instruction is as complex as establishing the need for it. The cost may be measured against that of other programs within the institution, or against costs for similar programs in other institutions (Powers, 1982), if administrators are fortunate enough to have consortial arrangements to share data across institutional boundaries and if the data are truly comparable. Student–faculty ratios, costs per credit hour, external funding patterns, and other quantifiable items may be used to place programs into a hierarchical list within any institution (Mingle and Norris, 1981). Nevertheless, such lists should be viewed with considerable caution.

A college or university that needs to decrease expenditures quickly may view the elimination of a high-cost program as a tempting solution, but the elimination costs also much be considered. What income will be lost as a result? What service courses of the program will have to be added elsewhere to support remaining programs? What are the intangible costs (Powers, 1982) (for example, decreased support from alumni and alumnae)? In fields like education, demographic trends indicate that the demand for college graduates may return to earlier levels in only a few years; will the cost of starting new programs at the end of this decade be greater or less than the cost of retaining programs through a temporary low-enrollment phase? Finally, timeliness is an important consideration: "Decisions to terminate programs should take into account. . . a vacancy in the leadership of a program, faculty vacancies resulting from an unusual pattern of retirements, resignations, or nonrenewals, or significant decreases in enrollment or in revenues" (Powers, 1982, p. 9). In short, the true cost of program maintenance or reduction cannot be calculated simply; even the calculation of a quantifiable variable like cost requires careful judgments.

Because definitions of institutional mission, measurements of particular programs against the mission, and standards of quality are so difficult to articulate, there is a danger that the weight of program reduction may fall too heavily, or even exclusively, on the criteria of demand and cost. To quantify these criteria, however, a number of critically important judgments have to be made: What is the reference group? What are the norms? Are shared data comparable? Are there particular circumstances (retirements, for instance) to be considered in certain programs?

Even when it is possible to develop reliable cost and need analyses, the issue of normative needs still remains. Higher education institutions that include both service and leadership in their missions have to define their "own view of society's educational needs without regard for whether the members of society see them in exactly the same way" (Mingle and Norris, 1981, p. 6). Private institutions obligate themselves, through charters and other acts of incorporation as nonprofit agencies, to assume positions of educational leadership with particular aims in relation to society. Most public institutions of higher education also declare their intent to be more than servants to current and foreseeable market needs. Thus, in most institutions, simple analyses of program costs, enrollment trends, and employment opportunities are insufficient standards for program planning and evaluation. Chief academic officers and deans are thereby impelled to develop a "composite picture" (Mingle and Norris, 1981), linking mission, quality, need, and cost as they develop guidelines for program planning, evaluation, or reduction.

The Process of Programmatic Reduction Reallocation

The first step in planning for reduction of academic programs is to establish the need to reduce. Budget shortfalls may take this decision from the hands of administrators and faculty and place it in the hands of legislators or trustees (Heydinger, 1982). Colleges and universities that have the opportunity and the time — after a period of planning and forecasting that involves faculty members to arrive at the same conclusion — are more likely to sustain faculty morale through subsequent stages of the process (Franklin, 1982).

If criteria for program planning and review are not already in place, it is essential to develop them, in consultation with faculty, before any programs are identified for review and possible elimination. Indeed, it is at this point that faculty members may be most helpful, since they are being asked to guide the standards for educational programs but are not required to assume the anticollegial position of identifying programs or faculty positions for elimination (Powers, 1982; Franklin, 1982). The roles of deans and faculty advisers in this process vary considerably: In some institutions it may be most appropriate for the chief academic officer to make clear that consensus is not expected and that faculty members are playing an advisory role (Franklin, 1982), while in others it may be possible for faculty "to assume a responsible role in the retrenchment process by being called on to ratify necessary retrenchment guidelines" (Powers, 1982, p. 10). Whichever arrangement is chosen, mutual understanding of the roles adopted is essential.

Once guidelines for evaluation of academic programs have been formulated, some institutions will involve all programs in a process of self-study and review (Heydinger, 1982), while others will use these same guidelines simply to identify programs of uncertain value that should be reviewed (Powers, 1982; Franklin, 1982). The choice of how to use guidelines depends on a number of factors: time available before decisions must be made, the process to be used, and purposes of reviews (whether they are undertaken purely to achieve retrenchment based on a program's past record in terms of centrality, quality, cost, and demand, or whether a second purpose is to reshape programs, as possible, to improve their future performance relative to these same criteria).

A process embracing universal review has the advantage of equity, a fundamental principle of collegiality, but also may strain the resources of the institution and reduce to unacceptable levels the amount of communication and consultation on particular programs that can reasonably occur. Selective review — or review of all programs, but over a period of years, when retrenchment is not the only or primary purpose — allows for more careful communication and consultation and exempts whole sectors of the institution from the time-consuming and anxiety-provoking process of self-study.

Establishing and maintaining the legitimacy of the review process itself will determine the choices made in particular settings. In some colleges and universities the participation of outside consultants may be required to reassure faculty and others of the adequacy of internal decision making (Franklin, 1982), a factor which would argue for selective review. Elsewhere, the review process may be credible only if it is universally applied, in which case there may be less opportunity for extensive consultation either inside or outside the institution, depending on the time available before decisions must be made.

Adequate communication about — and scrupulous adherence to — the process that is chosen may be even more important than the choice itself. According to Powers (1982, p. 9), "When a program is under scrutiny and, therefore, jeopardized, the most common cry of protest is that correct process is not being followed." Particularly when only certain programs have been selected for review on the basis of officially adopted criteria, and it is therefore understood that they have "obvious and incontestable defects," the "defenders will attack the review and evaluation process and sometimes the evaluators, as well" (Powers, 1982, p. 9). No amount of communication can guarantee the absence of confrontation, but time spent in explaining and clarifying the process is well invested.

Trustees or other governing boards play a crucial role in establishing the legitimary of the review process (Franklin, 1982; Powers, 1982). In institutions where reductions in faculty size have occurred with minimal disruption, the criteria for reduction and the process to be used have both been reviewed and endorsed by trustees.

Finally, the reduction procedures adopted need either to include clear statements about faculty and students in threatened programs or, when programs are discontinued, to refer to existing policies on the rights of students and tenured faculty members. Legal constraints on colleges and universities undertaking retrenchment procedures are well documented elsewhere (Eddy, 1981; Hendrickson, 1981; Mortimer, 1982; Powers, 1982). Even when they are not legally required to do so, administrators may wish to ensure that tenured faculty will either not be released or be given generous retraining stipends for moving to academic areas of greater need or be given priority to fill administrative vacancies as they occur. Creative early retirement plans may also be developed to soften the impact of retrenchment on faculty (Heydinger, 1982). Discontinuing programs also has an impact on students. Some may move to closely related programs, but a "program-by-program (and probably student-by-student) analysis is required to minimize injury" (Powers, 1982, p. 10). Perhaps phasing out a program will require several years to ensure that students have access to the courses they will need for completing their degrees.

Most of the literature on faculty reduction, reallocation, and retrenchment has focused on the traumas and legal constraints associated with shrinkage, but there are some potential benefits as well. Where these can be identified in advance, such benefits should be incorporated into reduction plans. For example, some of the resources saved through reduction may be directed toward salary raises for continuing faculty or toward improvement of research programs or facilities (Franklin, 1982, p. 35). Mingle and Norris (1981, p. 8) cite a study showing that "the most successful retrenchments cut deeply enough to meet immediate and projected shortfalls and also to mount new programs or enhance existing ones. It is this second order of cuts [beyond those required to balance the budget] which can be the positive side of retrenchment." The initial definition of the need for reduction will determine whether the aim is institutional survival or enhancement of institutional quality. Hence, the first step in planning the process for program reduction remains the most important.

Conclusions

For most institutions of higher education during the demographic downturns of the 1980s and the early 1990s, declining resources will require chief academic officers to play roles for which neither they nor faculty members have been prepared by the events of recent decades. A few fortunate CAOs may escape entirely the need to reduce instructional expenditures and simultaneously maintain the educational viability of their institutions, but most will need to reconsider not only the nature of their roles but also key concepts such as accountability, collegiality, leadership, and planning. In the process, these CAOs may have the chance to redefine such bedrock terms in the best interests of their institutions.

A favorite word of the 1970s — "accountability" — had a purely public meaning: Was higher education delivering what it promised? The term is being appropriated in this decade by faculty members who want to know if their CAOs are adequately protecting the interests of the instructional budget, which amounts to around a quarter of most institutions' expenditures. This definition of accountability within colleges and universities will require CAOs to work more closely with other senior officers of their institutions to ensure that the challenges of increasing revenues and decreasing expenditures are spread appropriately throughout the various administrative divisions.

Collegiality, another central term, may also acquire new meanings in the decade ahead. The term grew to maturity in institutions characterized by what Franklin (1982, p. 34) calls "atomistic governance and an overwhelmingly self-protective cultural milieu." In the past generation, those bound by ties of collegiality have watched the purchasing power of academic salaries decline, while deferred maintenance (and deferred purchasing of needed goods and services) has mounted. The definition of collegiality developed in the past generation will not serve the next one well; a recentering of the term on its original context of service and public accountability is needed.

Leadership in the next decade will also have to focus the energies of faculty and administrators on retaining what is best in higher education while numbers of traditional students decline and the flow of external resources to colleges and universities is erratic. In this environment, CAOs who assume that leadership means protection of the institutional budget against all other sectors of the institution will serve neither their faculties nor their institutions well.

Planning—if it is started in time—will remain the key to resolving the thorniest issues of reduction. The criteria and processes of retrenchment are strikingly similar to those for long-range planning, but the impact of these two processes on people and institutions is remarkably different. The difference is simply a question of whether the standards and procedures are developed by faculty and administrators before they are urgently needed or whether they are created and implemented in haste.

Realistic, long-range planning is clearly preferable, especially since programmatic cuts are demoralizing and across-the-board cuts are likely to reduce the institution's effectiveness. If institutional goals are clear, it should still be possible to "prune and use a scalpel now, rather than having to swing a hatchet later" (Ginsburg, 1982, p. 15). Planning for institutional quality—that is, for institutions that decide to do fewer things better while enhancing revenues and containing costs—is still a viable option when accountability, collegiality, and leadership prevail.

References

Bowen, H. R. "Effective Education at Reasonable Costs." In W. Godwin (Ed.), *Higher Education: Myths, Realities, and Possibilities.* Atlanta: Southern Regional Education Board, 1972.

Bowen, H. R. "Sharing the Effects: The Art of Retrenchment." *AAHE Bulletin,* September 1982, 10–13.

Bowen, H. R., and Douglass, S. K. "Cutting Instructional Costs." In W. Jellema (Ed.), *Efficient College Management.* San Francisco: Jossey-Bass, 1972.

Eddy, M. S. "Faculty Response to Retrenchment." *AAHE Bulletin,* June 1981, 7–10.

Franklin, P. "Duke University: Retrenchment Can Be Accomplished Without Alienating the University Community from Its Administration." *Educational Record,* 1982, 34–38.

Ginsburg, S. G. "120 Ways to Increase Income and Decrease Expenses." *Business Officer,* 1982, 14–16.

Hendrickson, R. M. "Legal Aspects of Faculty Reduction." San Francisco: Jossey-Bass, 1981.

Heydinger, R. B. "Using Program Priorities to Make Retrenchment Decisions: The Case of the University of Minnesota." Southern Regional Education Board offprint, 1982, pp. 2–8.

Meeth, L. R. *Quality Education for Less Money: A Sourcebook for Improving Cost Effectiveness.* San Francisco: Jossey-Bass, 1974.

Mingle, J. R. "Redirecting Higher Education in a Time of Budget Reduction." *SREB Issues in Higher Education,* 1982, *18,* 1–12.

Mingle, J. R., and Norris, D. M. "Colleges Respond to Decline: Resistance versus Adaptation." *SREB Issues in Higher Education,* 1981, *17,* 1–8.

Mortimer, K. P. "Procedures and Criteria for Faculty Retrenchment." *SREB Issues in Higher Education,* 1982, *18,* 6–7.

Newman, F. "Selecting the Effects: The Priorities of Retrenchment." *AAHE Bulletin,* 1982, 11–13.

Powers, D. R. "Reducing the Pain of Retrenchment." *Educational Record,* 1982, 8–12.

Christine A. Young has most recently been provost of Hood College.

*The chief academic officer needs to decide on appropriate
attitudes, issues, implementation strategies, and evaluative
criteria in dealing with the new technologies.*

Taking Advantage of Emerging Educational Technologies

J. Terence Kelly
Kamala Anandam

Higher education, like society in general, is in the midst of an awesome
infusion of technology that is threatening the traditional foundations of
academia. The threat is not so much whether the impact is positive or
negative; it is more the imminence of dramatic changes in the organizational arrangements by which teachers teach and students learn.
Although a number of colleges and universities operate much as they
did at the turn of the century — with the instructors and students
clustered in classroom groups — the emerging technology unquestion-
ably challenges this model.

   With its far-reaching implications for education, economics, and
ethics, computer technology represents the most provocative innovation that has ever been introduced in higher education. Much of the
philosophy and many of the assumptions and approaches that will be
developed in this chapter are applicable to other forms of technology,
but the context for our writing relates directly to computer technology.

   The chief academic officer must possess the leadership qualities
that will be able to harness and exploit the technology for maximum

D. G. Brown (Ed.). *Leadership Roles of Chief Academic Officers.* New Directions
for Higher Education, no. 47. San Francisco: Jossey-Bass, September 1984.

improvement of the learning climate. There are tragic stories of institutions that back in the late 1950s and the early 1960s began to equip classrooms and auditoriums with television sets, only to find that instructional personnel were uncommitted to the medium as an instructional tool, unfamiliar with how to use it, and, worst of all, not in philosophical agreement with the directions their institutions were taking. Unless substantive planning is undertaken, similar prospects are likely for computer technology.

Given the pervasiveness of technology and the precarious nature of decision making, staying at the cutting edge only where state-of-the-art hardware systems are concerned will not be prudent. Simply because the institution may lack the enhancement that vendors announce, and for which faculty clamor, is absolutely no reason to panic or feel that the institution is behind the times. Amazing new features are being added to computers at an astounding rate, and there seems to be no end to this growth. In some areas, keeping up with the new developments is more crucial than in others, and it is wise to recognize not only that students can learn on last year's models but also that they can adapt to working environments that have the newer technological advancements.

Assumptions About the Readers

To make this chapter as meaningful as possible, we have set forth our assumptions about our readers. If some of these assumptions are erroneous, we apologize.

1. We assume that our readers' interest in computer technology stems from the belief that, if properly applied, the technology can improve the teaching–learning environment. Our premise, therefore, is that the readers are interested in bettering the quality of learning, improving instructional methods, maximizing the economics of the instruction, and evaluating the learning outcomes. Furthermore, we assume that the driving force behind the interest in moving technology into a college or university learning environment is to discover the most effective applications of computer technology in concert with the most effective attributes of people.

2. Given the haphazard, piecemeal, and erratic means by which computer technology is emerging throughout our society, we assume that the chief academic officers are searching for a process to follow in developing or refining sensible plans for incorporating the technology within the institution.

3. Since we are addressing CAOs, we assume that from their experience as leaders in education these individuals recognize the need to internalize and evaluate the ideas presented in this chapter so that they can be accepted, adjusted, or rejected for individual settings.

4. Knowing the current economic condition of American higher education, we assume that our readers operate with limited resources in dealing with issues of computer technology. Reource management has been a constant juggling act in the life of CAOs; but now many factors come into sharper focus when one resorts to computer technology. These include the interplay of faculty role shifts, productivity emphasis, accountability demands, inordinate capital investment, development or maintenance of software, monitoring and management of people's access to hardware and software, and evaluation of teaching and teachers.

Our Beliefs and Biases About Educational Technology

Just as we must assume a point of view on the part of the reader, our readers need to be aware of our biases and perspectives, which follow.

1. *The use of technology is evolutionary.* We believe that we are in the midst of what Alvin Toffler (1980) calls "the third wave," meaning the technological revolution. No revolution has left the people it touched unchanged, but people rarely change as dramatically and rapidly as revolutionary inventions do. The products of the technological revolution change people to the extent that people use them. Therefore, even though technological inventions are revolutionary, we believe that their use will travel an evolutionary path.

2. *Humans should be in the foreground.* Men and women leading the technological revolution have emphasized the need to reduce the gap between innovations and their adoption. Closing the gap will depend, we believe, on considering people's needs, rather than on imposing technology on them.

3. *Learners need "mind storms" and "mind calms."* No one has escaped the sales pitch about the capabilities of computers—their speed, storage capacities, colors, touch screens, graphics, screen windows, and so on. For students, we are told, computers' capability of giving immediate feedback is impressive; but impressive for what? Memorizing facts? Giving impulsive responses, rather than considered answers? Following a path of random investigation monitored by visible consequences, instead of mapping out alternate strategies based on abstract

reasoning? The intensity of human activity at computer terminals cannot *always* be equated with human learning, either for all students or even for some. We believe that the use of technology should create "mind storms" as well as "mind calms," the former resulting in fearless exploration and the latter promoting self-validation and reflection. For "mind calms," immediate feedback is not essential and could be detrimental.

4. *Risk is inevitable.* The growth of technological inventions is mind-boggling, to say the least. How anyone can keep up with it and make sensible decisions is beyond human speculation; at best, we can venture into this arena only in a spirit of experimentation. Unfortunately, the technological revolution has come upon us all too suddenly, denying us the luxury of sizing up the situation adequately before making decisions. Consequently, we are bound to make decisions on the basis of our circumstances. Whatever decisions we make and whatever actions we take, we can be sure of one thing: Risk is inevitable when we are involved with technology. In terms of financial investments, the risk is obvious and important. What is less obvious but equally important is the risk concerning human resources, and we believe that recognizing these risks is crucial to leaders who are embracing technology. Recognition of a risk renders it a calculated risk.

5. *Cost effectiveness is subjective.* Quite often, educators attempt to apply the concept of cost-effectiveness to technological innovations. While cost savings and income benefits are tangible and measurable, we believe that cost-effectiveness is intangible and should therefore be assessed subjectively. For instance, if we introduce a computer workstation for $8,000 and lay off one instructor whose salary is $18,000, there is a cost savings. If, having introduced the workstation, we rent it out during holiday periods or provide services at night, there is an income benefit. But how do we measure cost-effectiveness? We see at least eight ways of answering that question: doing more work for the same cost (quantity), doing the work better for the same cost (quality), doing the work faster for the same cost (speed), doing the same work for the same cost (more positive emotional environment), doing more work for less cost, doing the work better for less cost, doing the work faster for less cost, and doing the same work for less cost. Of course, these directions all assume that definite base-line information is available for whatever comparison criterion has been selected—student's learning, student's motivation, faculty's commitment, administrator's

enthusiasm, institution's prestige, community's attitude, state support, or federal grants.

The unique circumstances of an institution, as well as its short-term and long-term goals, will determine what is cost-effective for that institution. Therefore, we have come to believe that cost-effectiveness is at least partly in the eye of the beholder.

Facilitating Factors and Negative Forces Influencing Leadership

Since this entire volume is addressing the CAOs at institutions of higher learning, it is not necessary to discuss leadership qualities per se, and so we will attempt to elaborate on facilitating factors and negative forces unique to leadership as it relates to educational technology.

Awareness of Issues. An awareness of issues, if not necessarily of their resolution, is a facilitating factor for capitalizing on technology. One issue centers on the cautionary adage, "Don't reinvent the wheel." While reinventing does represent duplication of efforts and expenditures, we would like to change this saying to "Assemble the wheel" and thus, once and for all, end the debate on reinventing the wheel. Each institution, we believe, needs to borrow whatever parts it can use, invent whatever additional parts it needs, and assemble the wheel to suit its own circumstances.

With the advent of microcomputers, a second issue of centralized versus distributed computing arises. To make things worse, many who clamored for stand-alone facilities are now suggesting local-area networks. In the coming years, the interface among and between computers — not computers themselves — will be the critical issue. How this issue will be settled at various institutions is not so much a function of technology as it is of the personalities and philosophies of the people involved in decision making.

Institutions do not have unchanging work forces. As institutional personnel move in and out, issues associated with technology take different turns, and institutions are likely to reinvest their time and effort in resolving them. Therefore, technological innovations should be considered as dynamic (not static), fluid (not rigid), and relative (not absolute). The shock of changes in personalities and philosophies will be the establishment of goals for educational technology, of principles and criteria governing choices, and of procedures for planning and implementing. The emphasis here is not on what to do but on how to do it.

The issue of immediate versus delayed success is tricky. Unless we carefully delineate what successes to expect and when to expect them, technological innovations may be abandoned before their potential is realized, particularly if potential users of the technology are not informed of the timeline for realizing expectations. We can expect to increase the success of technological innovation by use of a model presented elsewhere (Anandam and Kelly, 1982b). Among the major activities that our model associates with any technological innovation, we note that design and dissemination begin at the same time, but that dissemination is necessary over a longer time and is monitored and modified by evaluation. In a later section of this chapter, we shall discuss the role of evaluation in educational technology.

Toleration of Changes and Accommodation of Failures. Creating an academic climate that tolerates changes and accommodates failures facilitates the use of technology for instruction. We hasten to add that some changes have a fleeting existence: Just when people get used to them another change arrives. The uncertainty, ambiguity, and relativity of technology are not conducive to operational stability. Toffler (1980) contends that the coping strategies we acquired during the industrial revolution—regulation, manipulation, and coordination—will not help us with the information revolution. If we interpret Toffler correctly, the information revolution requires us to restructure the old leadership role in a known territory into a new role of social responsibility mapped onto the unknown domain. Anticipation, initiation, facilitation, and participation become the expressions of this new role. The focus on social responsibility helps academic leaders deemphasize power politics, minimize egoism and create a "lead and be led" environment, all of which tunes leaders into people's feelings and helps people tolerate changes.

Since risk is inevitable given involvement with technology, failures are also to be expected. It would be foolhardy to launch an innovation without anticipating the circumstances and chances of failure or planning for alternatives and backups. The rule of thumb is to consider every innovation as an experiment and give the people who are the prime experimenters full support, both moral and monetary. If the experiment fails, the moral support becomes even more crucial, and punitive measures are definitely ruled out.

Creative Financing: Reallocating Human Resources and Manipulating Budgets. One very positive factor that facilitates the role of academic officers in moving technology into institutions is the ability to say, "I'll find the money." This suggests that careful budget analysis can show ways to uncover or reallocate money. This is no new feat for the most astute academic officers, but again, because of pressures and the amounts of resources necessary for hardware and software acquisitions and for long-term maintenance of both, skills in manipulating the budget need to be fine-tuned. One way to facilitate equipment purchases is to find better ways in which human resources can be used. Sometimes this becomes a "chicken or egg" argument. Let us assume for a moment that thirty computer workstations could eliminate the need for two instructional slots. Can one accomplish this objective without already having the dollars to buy the thirty computer workstations? Even if money is available, will the computer workstations be totally maintenance free? We think not. It may be sensible, therefore, for CAOs to find ways of reorganizing instructional personnel, such that full-time instructors may be coupled with paraprofessional lab assistants or other lower-salaried personnel and still be able to facilitate learning in a more productive manner.

Another strategy for uncovering dollars is to consider the possibility of shifting from operating expenses to equipment purchases on a short-term basis. Often this approach is prohibitive, but managing with few operating funds for materials, supplies, and other normal expenses, while garnering extra money from around the institution, can facilitate equipment acquisition.

Because of financial constraints, it is necessary as never before that CAOs have more precise criteria and clear-cut methods for establishing institutional priorities over several years and for modifying priorities from year to year. For example, the need to strengthen data-processing training programs might be selected as a priority during the next three years, since the need for trained programmers is great. Let us say that certain decisions to acquire hardware are made in the first year, with the intention of expanding acquisitions in the next two years. Let us assume also that priorities shift to office careers in the second year and that funds are reallocated to accommodate this shift. Should such contingencies arise (and they do all the time), will the data processing department be able to carry on its activities during the second year with the money allocated in the first year? This is the kind of question that CAOs should answer for themselves when they are making decisions about computer technology.

Recognition of Role Shifts (Administrators and Faculty). The emergence of technology will clearly cause drastic changes in the roles and responsibilities of both faculty and administrators. One claim that seems very reasonable is that faculty may no longer be considered the prime deliverer of information. It should be recognized that some faculty in some situations may be least effective in dispensing information, but computers can simply do it better. Properly developed systems can deliver information, verify its accuracy, update it, and reinforce and individualize student learning. This suggests a rather dramatic shift for faculty members from being the primary givers of information to being facilitators of learning. In this new role, an instructor can monitor larger numbers of students, individualize instruction to a much greater degree than has ever been possible, and become an organizer, monitor, and evaluator of learning in more different ways than in the traditional classroom model.

Additionally, data generated through computer learning systems will compel faculty members to become responsible for understanding and analysis. Learning stages, for example, can be much better defined, identified, and, consequently, understood. Faculty who are the most adept at reading computer printouts or terminal displays, digesting student profiles, and understanding intake as well as output measures will become much more proficient and comfortable in working with a system approach to learning.

Administrators will also experience role shifts as more accurate and timely information is available for monitoring, evaluating, and modifying (as necessary) the learning environment. Strengths of existing academic programs, needs for redirection of curriculum emphasis, faculty problems, and constraints on learning become more apparent through computer-based information systems. A promising outgrowth of the availability of this information is that administrators can use technology to solve some of the problems that technology brings to light in the first place. For instance, computer-based education makes it possible to move students through different kinds of instructional programs according to learning style and learning speed, reorganize teaching–learning settings so that capabilities of faculty are appropriately matched to teaching tasks, focus on tangible information to evaluate faculty and help them realize their potential, and plan for administrative and organizational changes that will be conducive to partnerships among faculty, students, and computers for enhancement of learning.

Leadership Approaches

While it is too early to predict which approach will result in long-lasting impact, some leadership approaches for moving technology into the education arena seem to be emerging.

The Bombshell Approach. Several institutions have used what we refer to as the bombshell approach. A typical example of this approach is the declaration by a CAO that all students and all faculty will possess computer terminals or microcomputers by a particular date.

This approach has positive and negative outcomes. It certainly speaks in no uncertain terms of the institution's commitment to technology and of the belief that students and faculty will perform better with access to this technology. It commits the institution to an entirely different stance on bringing about change, but students and faculty may not be ready for such an approach. If they are not, some drastic consequences are probable. Moreover, without careful consideration of the questions related to selection and standardization of equipment and software and costs involved, some institutions may well exceed their tolerance level of financial stress.

The Supportive Approach. In the supportive approach, knowledgeable CAOs who recognize the need for moving computer technology into institutions take a step backward and find ways to prompt the faculty to take the intiative. These CAOs encourage faculty to attend seminars and bring in visiting experts to the campus. They also allow time for the faculty's interest to ripen. Once the stage is set, the CAO is quick to support faculty intiatives. The supportive approach is time-consuming and often leads to demands based on personal interests rather than on real institutional needs, and so the movement of technology into instruction may take place in spurts. Nevertheless, the supportive approach does tend to generate genuine interest from those who have caught on. On the whole, it is reassuring when time and care go into moving technology into the institution in a more cautious but perhaps also more sound way.

The Collaborative Approach. Collaboration is significant given the present financial crisis of educational institutions. Consortium arrangements already allow colleges and universities to share the costs of acquiring educational materials and equipment. With standard equipment, this type of sharing makes sense. Even if cost sharing is not feasible, coordinated buying saves money. In computer technology, mainframe facilities are sometimes established through shared resources, and computer processing is made available on site at the different institutions. In other cases, one institution, having bought the mainframe hardware, may choose to sell computer time and services to other institutions.

Software development for computer-based education represents another dimension of interinstitutional collaboration. This type of collaboration is instigated when common needs of several institutions come to light through international, national, state, and local organizations. For example, under the auspices of the League for Innovation in the Community College, Miami–Dade Community College recently completed the development of "Camelot: The Individualized Information System" on behalf of four United States institutions, as well as one in Canada and one in the United Kingdom. All these institutions contributed money to this joint venture. Eleven more institutions also participated in the project by field testing the system. Of course, such collaborative efforts not only reduce the financial burden on any one institution but also improve the quality of the end product.

Collaboration between industry and education is becoming more popular as industries look to educational institutions to supply trained personnel for employment. This situation is very attractive to educators, particularly when industries are willing to supply hardware in return for training sound programs. Computer programming, architecture, engineering, electronics, office careers, and business are all areas that have gained from this type of collaboration.

Quite a different trend — and a positive one — is also appearing in education and industry. This trend is directed toward developing a computer software for educational settings. Ploch (1984) describes some of the partnerships between educational institutions and computer hardware vendors. The time is right for educational institutions to lead the way in software development and its uses. Every institution should examine how it can attract the collaboration of industry. This collaboration is important for three reasons: to procure needed hardware and money, to satisfy business needs, and to shape the direction of technology itself for meeting the needs of educational institutions.

The Capitalization Approach. Being in the right place at the right time is the essential ingredient of the capitalization approach. Opportunities may include a generous hardware offer by a commercial vendor, a substantial external grant, bequests to support new technology, and so on. Under most conditions these events are unplanned and unexpected. Nevertheless, they do present real opportunities, and if all other elements are equal, they should be seized.

Seeking external funds through competitive grants or endowments is another aspect of the capitalization approach. It may be wise to designate one or two individuals at the institution to work specifically toward these possibilities.

Building up financial resources is not the only target in the capitalization approach; enhancing human resources is equally important. Exchange-teacher programs, visiting-professor programs, distinguished-professor seminars, professional leaves, sabbaticals, and other programs may be directed toward moving technology into the academic mainstream. While these directions represent use of existing mechanisms, another exciting possibility of enhancing human resources is to fill a faculty position with someone familiar with the applications of technology to a particular discipline.

The Voodoo Approach. Some institutions seem to have had very systematic and rational ways in which computers were incorporated. When we try to investigate the factors allowing this phenomenon, sooner or later we find out that there is no logical explanation: No one seems to understand how it occurred, and even CAOs are at a loss to identify all the forces and factors that brought about the changes. A conglomeration of events — external grants, successful faculty initiatives, and alumni endowments, among other factors — has produced a highly desirable environment in the absence of a rational plan or a systematic, organized method of incorporating the technology. While this phenomenon may occur at some institutions, we do not recommend relying on it as a desirable approach, but if things do seem to happen by voodoo, accept them.

Evaluating Technological Innovation

Instructional uses of computers can be classified as learning about computers, learning through computers, learning with computers, and learning with computer support. Learning about computers is the most visible area of instructional computing. It is commonly known as data processing. Learning through computers is more popularly called computer-assisted instruction, in which a student interacts directly with the computer for drill and practice, diagnostic testing, tutorials, simulation, and problem solving. Learning with computers involves discipline-specific aids to learning, such as computer-assisted design in architecture or spread sheets in accounting. Learning with computer support is known as computer-managed instruction, and it is expanding quietly in higher education, often without any particular notice taken of the computer's role.

Which emphasis is best? There are few topics more elusive than evaluating the use of technology in education. The elusiveness stems from improper technological taxonomy; a failure to understand what, when, and why to evaluate. Given this ambiguity, the question of technology's cost-effectivness is premature, and hurriedly sought answers have yielded not only conflicting findings but also hasty decisions.

Bloom (1971, p. 117) discusses two roles of evaluation — formative and summative. Formative evaluation pertains to the process of developing a program, while summative evaluation focuses on the completed program. Formative evaluation is "the use of systematic evaluation in the process of curriculum construction, teaching, and learning for the purpose of improving any of these three processes." Most evaluations of technological innovations have failed to include formative evaluation and so are handicapped by mixed findings.

Evaluative studies, furthermore, focus on different objectives — economics, productivity, faculty acceptance, or student motivation and performance. All are valid objectives worthy of evaluation, but they will provide meaningful information of practical significance only if they are considered in the context of the three phases of innovation we have described elsewhere (Anandam and Kelly, 1982a) as "the three E's" — extensiveness, effectiveness, and endurance. Extensiveness refers to how widespread the use of technology is in education; effectiveness refers to improvement in human (faculty and student) satisfaction and in student motivation, retention, and learning; and endurance refers to the long-lasting continuation of an innovation. Technological innovation is neither easy nor quick; therefore, evaluation in the area of technology and education should be looked at in a special way. Extensiveness, effectiveness, and endurance represent three aspects of an innovation diffusion, each of which requires different parameters for evaluation. There has to be extensiveness before there can be measured effectiveness, and effectiveness has to be established before the innovation will endure. The research questions that should be posed for each of these aspects are very different. While an institution is engaged in extensiveness, questions of effectiveness are rather premature, and should they be pursued, the innovation is doomed to failure even before it starts. As we engage in extensiveness, we ask: What kind of leadership promotes extensive adaptation? What kind of effort is needed to promote extensiveness? When we move into the effectiveness area, we deal with these questions: What is actually learned through the computer or with the computer? Which kinds of students learn better with computers? What kinds of learning are promoted through computers? In terms of endurance, we are looking at the structure of rewards, both for the faculty and for students. When the novelty of an innovation fades into the background, what are the enduring features that make it continue? These three types of questions are important concepts in evaluation. Extensiveness, effectiveness, and endurance all have their own purposes and require different types of evaluation at different stages.

Conclusion

We are all part of the technological revolution, a still-ambiguous phenomenon in which uniform methods are antithetical to creativity. We hope we have presented a model for the process of enhancing academic leadership for emerging educational technology. We had to develop the process model with our own content—assumptions, beliefs, facilitating factors, possible approaches, and sensible evaluation. We thought this development was necessary to describe the process concretely rather than abstractly and to set the stage for thinking about assumptions and beliefs. We hope we also have helped identify the facilitating factors, negative influences, appropriate approaches, and meaningful evaluations that are applicable to particular institutions.

References

Anandam, K., and Kelly, J. T. "Evaluating the Use of Technology in Education." *Journal of Educational Technology Systems,* 1982a, *1* (10), 21–31.
Anandam, K., and Kelly, J. T. "Teaching and Technology: Closing the Gap." *Technological Horizons in Education,* 1982b, *10* (2), 84–90.
Bloom, B. S., and others. *Handbook on Formative and Summative Evaluation of Student Learning.* New York: McGraw-Hill, 1971.
Ploch, M. "Micros Flood Campuses." *High Technology,* 1984, *4* (3).
Toffler, A. *The Third Wave.* New York: Bantam, 1980.

J. Terence Kelly is vice-president for education at Miami–Dade Community College.

Kamala Anandam is a professor at Miami–Dade Community College.

*Missions will change in a future that will inevitably be
different from the past.*

Goals, Academic Direction,
and Faculty Development

Maurice Glicksman

Institutional Goals

Higher education has increased its pervasive role in our society
during recent decades. The American people have a high regard for
the purpose of, and the participants in, higher education, and the
percentage of Americans past the age of eighteen who have attended
institutions of higher education has been steadily, even dramatically,
increasing (32 percent according to the 1980 Census, as compared to
17 percent in 1960 and 10 percent in 1940).

In the past, colleges and universities served mainly to educate
an elite among the American population. Many benefited from the
liberal arts character of their education, and many were also enabled to
enter into professions. For almost all, the four years of college (plus additional periods, as needed, for professional training) seemed to satisfy
the need for formal education. Since colleges and universities now are
serving a large fraction of the population (about half of our young people now spend some of their time after age eighteen in colleges or
universities), it is appropriate to examine the role and responsibility of

D. G. Brown (Ed.). *Leadership Roles of Chief Academic Officers.* New Directions
for Higher Education, no. 47. San Francisco: Jossey-Bass, September 1984.

such institutions in providing educational services to the population as a whole beyond the traditional years of college attendance.

Many graduates over the past decade or so have left our institutions believing that they could benefit from studying areas they had no opportunity to explore sufficiently in college. There has been obvious growth of informal and formal educational opportunities; examples include short courses at universities and colleges, extracurricular courses taught at public and private institutions for nearby residents, and tutorial programs involving the use of film, video, or computer-stored material. It is also true that our knowledge base is increasing so rapidly that many graduates must actively continue and expand study throughout their professional lives in order to practice their professions in a satisfactory manner. These needs are being recognized by the corporate world, which has continued to increase its investment in the training of its personnel. A number of corporations provide educational institutions for their own employees.

An increasingly important, related field is the commercial supply of information (much of it in the form of data bases) to individuals and organizations. Although this phenomenon could be considered an extension of the traditional role of book and magazine publishers, publishers have not been the pioneers in providing these services to the public.

Colleges and universities have tried to do two things well: to bring college-age students to a satisfactory understanding of themselves and the world in which they live and to serve society through dedication to the search for new understanding—the truths—of the world. But such a brief connection with young people will not suffice for the rapidly changing world, both because of explosive increases in information and, more important, because of continuing substantial changes in our understanding. The opening of minds to the potential of the future takes place on our campuses, and the long-term devotion to developing those minds should not be transferred to other places without universities and colleges examining how they might take part in this process and benefit society as well as themselves.

I propose that universities seriously consider modifying their mission. We should offer admission to qualified graduates of secondary schools, but not just for the normal, four-year baccalaureate programs; we should offer individuals, on a continuing basis, the opportunity to continue their educational experience beyond the baccalaureate degree period. We should also agree to provide our graduates with access to our libraries and other collections of information (including art and music), as well as to faculty and staff for assistance in the continuing quest for better understanding of our society as it develops. Of course, such services would be provided in return for payment, as is the case now for tuition and fees charged to students in residence.

Industries that have been developed to meet a given need have often flourished at first, but then decayed after perceiving that mission as their only one. Industries that have thrived on a long-term basis have also recognized the need to spend some of their resources on a continuing study of what they are doing and why, a study that often involves support for primary research. Higher education has done very little self-study. I believe we need to devote much more attention to research on the educational and scholarly process. As we develop a better understanding of human cognition, a better base for studying individual intellectual and scholarly development is becoming available. The very individual nature of the educational process has led many of us to assume that the system is too complex for research. The autonomy and individuality of faculty members has also discouraged study of what is being done and of how it can be done differently and better. Nevertheless, increasing availability and use of technical aids to education and research on our campuses can provide an opportunity for meaningful and effective studies. Institutions' motivation to consider means of improving educational effectiveness ("productivity") should also justify the investment of scarce resources in developing more basic educational research activities. I would urge institutions of higher education to take the lead in this process.

Academic Direction

Changes in academic direction take place slowly. Most institutions set up new departments or change their curricular policies only after detailed study and long deliberation. Such caution in modifying a system that has a long time-constant (it may be thirty-five years or more before a newly tenured faculty member retires) is essential to the health of higher education. I discuss two approaches here to change in academic programs; I have encouraged their development during this past decade and hope they will be seen as important to consider in the coming decade as well.

The first approach is the encouragement of scholarship and teaching at the "edge" of current disciplines. This century has seen the growth and entrenchment of the departmental structure at universities and colleges. Radical experiments involving the abolition of such structures have not been embraced warmly by the large majority of institutions. In an environment where increasing the faculty seems to be possible for only a few institutions now and perhaps a possibility for more at the turn of the century, we need to encourage exploration and vitality through the support of interdisciplinary ventures. In the past, these have been the seeds of the new disciplines and departments, but their development is inhibited by lack of the flexibility that is possible only with growing faculties. Methods for nurturing interdisciplinary trends (along with rigorous review of their academic quality as they develop) are, I believe, essential for the future health of academic life.

At Brown University we have encouraged the establishment of interdisciplinary programs and centers. These may be focused on research and scholarly work, but should also include teaching in an integral way. Such interdisciplinary groups at Brown in the humanities, arts, and sciences have grown in number over the past seven years, such that now their number is comparable to the number of departments. Several have flowered into new departments; several others have proved valuable, but not permanently so, and have been phased out. Encouraging these activities has stimulated creative involvement of faculty in exploring new ideas and connections. In a time of scarce resources, the institutional investment has been difficult to make, but the individual human investment has been so great that the institution has had to stretch itself to respond. Faculty and students respond positively and enthusiastically, and the potential of this approach for the future merits serious consideration by other institutions.

The second approach is the broadening of our educational horizons. Our world is smaller now than it was several decades ago. Our contact with other cultures, on the individual as well as the national front, is obvious and so is the importance of better mutual understandings. Yet our institutions of higher education have been slow to develop programs to foster such understanding in students. There seem to be two ways our programs can be improved to carry out this important task. It is essential to provide faculty and courses to introduce our students to other societies and cultures, with perspectives and values differing significantly from the generally Western emphasis of many of our current academic programs. Efforts to provide broader but no less rigorous curricula will take time, since this goal also requires training sufficient numbers of faculty via graduate programs in these areas. But I believe such an approach must be enthusiastically pursued if our universities and colleges are to serve our students and society well.

As important as such academic development is, there is another important key to providing a vital experience of other cultures for our students. We need to develop, as an integral part of our programs, the expectation that students will study and live in other societies during a portion of their college years. It is important for them to go where they will also be able to continue their academic development — to universities abroad that will encourage American students to live in the indigenous cultural and social environment while continuing their studies. Many of our institutions do encourage students to study abroad, but there has been little initiative to build this in as part of the American institution's standard curriculum. At Brown we have made a start by establishing joint programs with universities in many nations around the world. We also need to integrate this programs into our regular academic curriculum and impress on our students the key role this program can play in their education. This is a challenge for the 1990s.

Faculty Development

Most of the nation's universities and colleges went through a major expansion of their faculties in the 1960s and into the 1970s, as a result of increased enrollments during that period. This growth was followed by a leveling off (if not a decline) in the past decade, and now there is a demographic "bulge" in the age distribution of our faculties. Although we expect to see some slight increase in enrollments at the very end of this century, we do not expect anywhere near the growth we have had. What we will see, however, is a large number of faculty retiring in the 1990s. Even if we can replace all these faculty (a possibility dependent also on an adequate supply from graduate programs), we will continue to see varying rates of retirement and hiring over the next several decades as a result of the oscillatory age distribution built in by rapid expansion.

The system of graduate education has difficulty adjusting quickly to such variations; study for the Ph.D. takes five or six years past the baccalaureate. Thus, Ph.D. production may well be at a minimum when increased supply is required.

There is no easy solution to this challenge. We could encourage the overstaffing of departments, particularly in areas that have a large oversupply of highly creative individuals with new Ph.D.s, and decrease teaching responsibilities for each faculty member. This approach would require major additional funding, and I know of no evidence to indicate that it is necessary for the future health of many disciplines. A highly selective use of such a mechanism (either with oversized departments built up by a steady addition of young people or with adjunct research institutions attached to departments of normal size) should be considered carefully for areas with particularly critical demographic problems.

The inertia of our system is also displayed in the capabilities of faculty. I have already noted the importance of making the curriculum more pertinent to the cultural, economic, and political diversity of the world, and that this will entail changes in the kinds of faculty in our institutions. The world is also undergoing rapid technolgical changes, and their impact is already heavy for information supply and communications/computer technology applications in teaching and research. Many campuses are seeing a large influx of computers being used by students, faculty, and staff. There is currently a large demand on the institutions to provide training in computer literacy, not only for students but also for faculty and staff. This demand will continue for some years; it will be more difficult initially because of rapid changes in the available technology.

My own view is that eventually (in the 1990s) this technology will be as much a part of the environment as the telephone, the television, and the automobile are now. Understanding general principles will be helpful and important for all, while detailed familiarity will not, but the impact of the new technology can lead to substantive differences in the way we teach and do research. The participants in the process (students, faculty, and staff) will need to adopt a changed set of technical aids and adapt to the changing world.

Concluding Comments

My comments have been selective; there are many other questions and challenges that could be presented. I am reminded of the perceptive observation of O'Neill (1982), that previous predictions of the future underestimated the pace of technological change and overestimated the pace of social and political change. We are faced with rapid change and the need to respond in timely fashion with appropriate organizational and social modifications. Life should surely be interesting for the academic administrator in such an environment.

Reference

O'Neill, G. K. *Two Thousand and Eighty-One: A Hopeful View of the Human Future.* New York: Simon & Schuster, 1982.

Maurice Glicksman is provost of Brown University.

The Notre Dame Long-Range Plan indicates the range of issues comprehensive planning must address.

The Notre Dame Long-Range Plan

Timothy O'Meara

In the fall of 1980, Father Theodore M. Hesburgh, president of the University of Notre Dame, asked me to undertake a study embracing all parts of the university with respect to the university's priorities for the present decade.

In anticipation of the assignment, I had held a four-day retreat the previous summer with my advisory committee of deans. During a series of intense discussions, we considered various alternative strategies for the study and named it Priorities and Commitments for Excellence (PACE). On returning to campus and receiving the assignment, my first step was to appoint a central advisory committeee consisting of a group of distinguished scholars and departmental leaders drawn from each of the colleges and the law school and my advisory deans. Every aspect of the study, including the final report itself, was highly influenced by this committee. Members sought the views of the entire university community. They met with constituencies that included the faculties of all academic departments, student affairs, representative groups, students, and alumni, and they contributed to successive drafts of the report. In the end, the committee unanimously

D. G. Brown (Ed.). *Leadership Roles of Chief Academic Officers.* New Directions for Higher Education, no. 47. San Francisco: Jossey-Bass, September 1984.

supported all aspects of the final document except the approach that was taken with social centers, as explained in the text of the report.

While the committee made major and fundamental contributions to PACE, I wrote the final draft of the report and must bear full responsibility for its contents. I submitted the report to the president early in winter 1982, and it received wide circulation throughout the Notre Dame community.

Father Hesburgh forwarded the report to the board of trustees, and the trustees discussed it extensively at a meeting the following spring. In keeping with their tradition of emphasizing principles rather than intervening in management, the board then issued a statement citing principles, either explicit or implicit in the PACE Report, to which the board then wished to subscribe. The statement of the board appears at the end of this chapter.

The report immediately began to fulfill its goal as a blueprint for the University's future. Several recommendations were implemented almost simultaneously with the Report's distribution. A university curriculum committee appointed in March of 1983 began to meet regularly under the leadership of the associate provost. A committee on responsible alcohol use was in operation by May of the same year and submitted its findings the following March. The renovation of two buildings to provide better social facilities was completed in 1983, an honors program for a select group of freshmen was inaugurated in the fall of 1983, and by fiscal year 1983–1984 salaries of assistant and associate professors were well into number-one American Association of University Professors (AAUP) rankings, with salaries of full professors also increasing. In January 1984 the vice-president for development invited a wide spectrum of university administrators to make concrete suggestions for determining funding priorities on the basis of PACE recommendations. A timetable was drawn up for the university's next major fund drive, targeting major areas of endowment and funding. In February 1984 the university announced a $4 million addition to the law school and the construction of a life sciences building. Other PACE recommendations have come to serve as operational guidelines, particularly in such areas as faculty recruitment, affirmative action, departmental review plans, and environmental changes (academic, social, and religious).

Of all the issues addressed in the report, the role of research and means of strengthening the university's Catholic character involved the most vigorous debate. These are still salient issues in university, college, and departmental discussions. One issue that had received insufficient attention soon became evident—computing. Even as the report was being printed, plans were being proposed and approved for the role and replacement of the university's mainframe computer, a long-range plan was being submitted for a universitywide computer network system, and an investigation was being made into the availability of on-campus personal computers.

A study of this magnitude requires tremendous investment of time and talent. It is outdated almost as soon as the findings are committed to a report. As a process to involve and inform a large segment of the university community and as a prod to progress, however, its rewards are well worth the effort. Perhaps more important than the report itself are the intangible benefits that result over an extended period of time when colleagues grapple with issues of utmost importance to their future and that of the institution. Shared enthusiasm, close friendships, and especially faith and hope that an undertaking of this kind expresses in the future of the university should also not be underestimated.

Highlights of the Report of the Provost to the President

Our purpose in this report is to think through anew the mission of the University, to consider the state of the University today, to consider our potential for the decade ahead, and to make specific recommendations on how that potential might be achieved. All the recommendations of the report can be condensed into these three:

- We must excel as a university in the full sense of the word, actively engaged in teaching and research
- We must maintain our Catholic identity
- We must remain conscious of and faithful to our mission in all our actions and decisions.

The mission of the University of Notre Dame is to be influential in the enrichment of culture, society, and the church:

- through the education of young men and women as concerned and enlightened citizens with a religious, a Christian and, more specifically, a Catholic, sense of values
- through advanced education in doctoral studies and the professional schools
- through education reaching beyond the campus to our alumni, to the nation, and to the church
- and through creative and scholarly contributions to the arts and sciences, technology, the professions and public service.

Recommendation 1. It is recommended that the provost with the approval of the president, appoint a university curriculum committee to report and make recommendations to the Academic Council on the following matters:

- the overall structure of the undergraduate curriculum
- the general education requirements
- the role of philosophy and theology in the general education requirements
- academic standards
- academic advising and career counseling.

Recommendation 2. In pursuit of excellence in doctoral studies and research, of maintaining continuity in scholarship and research, of reducing the number of new doctorates in certain areas while increasing the quality and number in others, it is recommended that:

- programs of marginal quality be suspended
- strong programs be reinforced
- risks be taken in starting new programs of high potential
- flexibility be exercised in the allocation of resources, in the size of stipends, and in the use of postdoctoral fellows and professional specialists to take the place of graduate students in research
- departments concentrate their research interests in a small number of programs of large enough critical mass
- scholarship and research be expected from all departments, including those without graduate programs
- doctoral students be supported primarily to develop doctoral studies, not to assist in the teaching mission of the university
- vigorous recruitment and placement programs be introduced and supported
- high standards be exercised in candidacies, in assigning thesis advisors, and in approving theses.

Recommendation 3. It is recommended that a substantial number of endowed doctoral fellowships be established by 1990, each with an endowment sufficient to yield tuition, a competitive stipend, and research expenses for a twelve-month appointment.

Recommendation 4. It is similarly recommended that a substantial number of endowed advanced fellowships be established for use in the law, business, master of divinity, and other terminal professional programs.

Recommendation 5. It is recommended that the university associate itself with a small number of universities of high potential located in developing countries and assist in their pursuit of excellence through faculty exchanges and graduate studies.

Recommendation 6. The following general principles should apply to all centers and institutes of the University:

- centers and institutes should contribute to the mission of the university, be integral parts of the university's operation, and provide interface between its academic units and society
- their contributions should be through education, research, and innovative service, and not through advocacy
- they should be financially independent (except for short-term start-up money), with funding that can support an operation compatible with the goals of excellence of the university.

Recommendation 7. It is recommended that the provost appoint a committee to explore the feasibility of strengthening and developing programs for Catholic educators in management, research, instruction, subject matter, and religious education.

Recommendation 8. It is recommended that the university's involvement in continuing education follow these general principles and forms of action:

- programs in continuing education at Notre Dame have a national and an international appeal
- programs in continuing education for alumni be developed
- programmatic development and responsibility be separated from management of facilities
- programs involving academic credit be under the deans of the appropriate schools and colleges
- programs not involving academic credit be under the dean of continuing education when sponsored by organizations outside the university, under the Notre Dame sponsoring unit otherwise
- a seed fund be established to experiment with new programs for credit in continuing education
- the provost appoint a committee for continuing education, consisting of the dean of continuing education as well as other deans and directors, to advise the dean of continuing education on policy matters relative to programmatic criteria and quality, and priority of access to facilities
- faculty participation be treated as consulting, and faculty remuneration be within broad and competitive guidelines
- continuing education as a whole, though not necessarily in each of its activities, be financially self-sufficient.

Recommendation 9. It is recommended that the university re-examine the role of computer science in the university and the need for an academic unit dedicated to this general area.

Recommendation 10. It is recommended that a committee consisting of members of the two colleges — Arts and Letters and Science — be formed to encourage cooperation between the colleges on educational matters in the arts and sciences. A good starting point might be consideration of the creation of an honors program in the arts and sciences.

Recommendation 11. It is recommended that, in the course of the next seven years, the university, with the assistance of internal and external reviewers, undertake a comprehensive and confidential review of each of its academic departments, centers, and institutes, as well as the library, in the context of the pursuit of excellence and the overall mission of the university, with a subsequent summary report to the academic council in each case.

Recommendation 12. It is recommended that strong departments continue to be strengthened. It is further recommended that, rather than try to improve all departments simultaneously, the university focus on one or two departments at a time where standards are significantly raised and additional resources are provided under the special attention of the chairman, the dean, the vice-president for advanced studies, and the provost.

Recommendation 13. It is recommended that the university consider the Five-Year Development Program as a goal to be attained and, with this in mind, strive to double the present endowment of the library by 1990.

Recommendation 14. It is recommended that strong collections be strengthened. It is further recommended that the library not try to improve the entire collection simultaneously, but rather focus on collections related to those academic disciplines which are being strengthened in the university at the time.

Recommendation 15. It is recommended that the present strength of the press be assured and its influence expanded by establishing an appropriate endowment to insure core funding.

Recommendation 16. It is recommended that the university pursue the construction of a modern classroom building equipped with advanced educational media facilities and technology.

Recommendation 17. It is recommended that the university strive to find donors for two facilities: the first a life science resource center; and the second, an addition to the law school.

Recommendation 18. It is recommended that the university extend the successful renovation and maintenance program, currently in operation in the halls, to all academic buildings on campus. It is further recommended that the associate provost, with the assistance of the dean of administration, be involved in long-range plans for this program, including specific needs, projected annual costs, and recommendations as to possible sources of funding.

Recommendation 19. It is recommended that the associate provost and the vice-president for advanced studies, on the advice of each of the deans, prepare a long-range plan for the maintenance, renovation, and replacement of educational and research equipment. This plan should include specific needs, projected annual costs, and recommendations as to possible sources of funding.

Recommendation 20. In the interest of stimulating research of high quality at the university, it is recommended that:

- the vice-president for advanced studies be provided with a budget from gifts and endowment to stimulate research
- soft money for academic-year salaries for teaching and research faculty continue to be requested in all proposals in proportion to the research being performed
- the funds so obtained not be used for academic-year salaries but rather be channeled into a special fund to be used to stimulate research; first priority on the use of this special fund be given to transitional support and to those investigators who have contributed to the fund
- the concept of released time be discontinued for fractions of awards under 50 percent of salary
- the above changes in the use of soft money and released time be accomplished following a five-year schedule.

Recommendation 21. It is recommended that the university continue to foster a faculty environment in which:

- the intellect may range with the utmost freedom
- religion may enjoy an equal freedom
- teaching and research are cultivated in concert
- committed and dedicated Catholics predominate
- committed and dedicated persons of all faiths participate fully and equally
- the Congregation of Holy Cross participate more actively and in greater number through teaching, research, and administration
- sisters, brothers, and priests of other congregations and

dioceses also give witness to the community of faith by their presence on campus.

Recommendation 22. In the pursuit of academic excellence and of a better distribution of women, minorities, and Catholics on the faculty, it is recommended that:

- linkages be established with universities having strong doctoral and postdoctoral programs by systematically inviting their faculty for lectures, and by having our chairmen and deans systematically visit their departments prior to appointment time each year
- more positions be filled above the entry level so that candidates will have had enough time to prove themselves academically and find their moral and religious values
- there be much greater flexibility in moving positions from subdiscipline to subdiscipline during a search
- appointments be postponed when strong candidates cannot be found in a particular year
- the same high standards of assessment be observed in the pursuit of affirmative action appointments
- resources and positions be made available through endowment to assist in attracting more outstanding women and minorities to the faculty.

Recommendation 23. In the interest of sustaining and developing the Catholic character of the university, it is recommended that:

- the Congregation of Holy Cross put continued, indeed stronger, emphasis on the intellectual life and on academic careers in teaching and research
- this emphasis be primarily, but not exclusively, in the areas of philosophy and theology
- the university give special consideration in personnel decisions to the unique role which the Holy Cross community plays in the total endeavor of the university
- this consideration be consistent with prevailing standards of excellence.

Recommendation 24. As an aid to faculty recruitment and recognition, it is recommended that the university continue to seek endowed professorships. It is further recommended that:

- the endowment level for a professorship be examined periodically and set at an appropriate competitive amount
- in the interest of flexibility in recruiting the most distin-

guished scholars, donors be encouraged not to locate endowed professorships permanently in specific disciplines

- the university consider various strategies, such as simultaneously filling a cluster of chairs in an area already noted for its strength or potential, to obtain maximum impact in the pursuit of scholarly excellence.

Recommendation 25. Standards for promotion and tenure must be raised gradually but steadily as the university continues to develop as a major university.

Recommendation 26. It is recommended that the university achieve a number-one AAUP rating in each of the professional ranks by 1985.

Recommendation 27. It is recommended that the provost establish a committee to study the quality of undergraduate intellectual life on campus and make concrete recommendations for its continued improvement. Their work should be coordinated and integrated with that of the University Curriculum Committee and the Arts and Sciences Committee.

Recommendation 28. It is recommended that undergraduate enrollment be maintained at the projected figure of 7,300 during the 1980s. It is further recommended that during the academic year 1983–1984, the university re-evaluate the matter of proportion of men to women in the undergraduate student body in light of our experiences with coeducation. Finally, it is recommended that any changes in this proportion be accomplished without allowing the undergraduate enrollment, men and women, to exceed 7,300.

Recommendation 29. In the interests of maintaining and improving academic quality by enlarging the pool of applicants, of maintaining a student body with diversified economic backgrounds, and of significantly increasing minority enrollment, it is recommended that the university seek to increase endowment for undergraduate student aid threefold by 1990. It is further recommended that the present policy of using only endowment income for financial aid be continued.

Recommendation 30. In view of the important role that can and should be played by rectors in the education of Notre Dame students, it is recommended that:

- the duties, prerogatives, and reporting responsibilities of rectors be clearly defined by the Office of Student Affairs and clearly understood by the rectors
- high standards be exercised in appointments and renewals

- the university give preferential treatment to Holy Cross
- this preferential treatment be consistent with prevailing standards of excellence
- rectors be provided with adequate staff for servicing and maintaining their halls
- resources be made available to accomplish these ends.

Recommendation 31. It is recommended that Campus Ministry continue its role in:

- developing campus liturgy
- counseling and ministry
- raising the level of social conscience in the community and play a greater role in:
- addressing matters of faith
- addressing matters of individual and personal conscience.

Recommendation 32. In the interests of relieving overcrowding in the older halls and, where possible, creating additional common space; of providing alternative living arrangements for selected seniors; of alleviating housing needs for more of our transfer students; and of responding to the needs of men graduate students, it is recommended that alternative housing arrangements, including townhouse complexes, be pursued for selected seniors and for men graduate students.

Recommendation 33. In the interest of improving the quality of student life on campus, it is recommended that the following program be pursued:

- satellite social centers, similar to the Oak Room, be created in other parts of the campus
- Washington Hall be renovated, be made more comfortable, and be made available to the student body for academic, cultural, and social activities
- a central part of the campus, such as an area containing Washington Hall, LaFortune, and the Center for Social Concerns, be designated for the development of a cluster of social and cultural centers
- conceptual designs be sought from architects with established reputations in developments of this sort
- special emphasis be placed on the aesthetic qualities of the overall design
- special emphasis be placed on the funcitonal use and the aesthetic appeal of interior space
- the design take into account the renovation of existing facilities and the building of new ones

- on acceptance of the design by the university, a special priority be given to finding donors and making the design become a reality.

Recommendation 34. To fulfill Notre Dame's responsibility to its students and to the community in promoting the responsible use of alcohol, its recommended that:

- the provost, with the approval of the president, appoint a committee of administrators, faculty, rectors, and students to draw up a public statement on responsible drinking; to consider whether present practices and policies on alcohol are conducive to responsible drinking; and to recommend new policies where appropriate.

Recommendation 35. In the interest of maintaining the integrity of our intercollegiate athletic programs, it is recommended that:

- in the recruitment of prospective athletes, the university be subject to standards agreed upon by peer institutions and codified in the rules of appropriate collegiate associations
- in admission to the university, the same general criteria be applied to all students, including potential participants on intercollegiate teams
- student athletes be regarded first and foremost as students
- student athletes take a normal course of studies and be expected to graduate in four years
- student athletes live in regular student housing amidst other students and not in isolated groups
- the university compete only with those schools which share its ideals for intercollegiate athletics.

Recommendation 36. It is recommended that long-range plans be developed and continually updated in the areas of academic computing and administrative data processing. This planning function should be assigned to the assistant provost for computing, who will be assisted by the Committee on Computing Policy and the Users Committee on Computing.

Recommendation 37. It is recommended that a policy be developed to insure a review process for the acquisition of computers. the review process should consider the question of compatibility in the light of overall university capabilities and needs.

Recommendation 38. Recognizing that the need for large, general-purpose academic computing will continue in the decade of the eighties, and recognizing the increased role of distributed systems, it is recommended that a re-evaluation be made of the support provided by the mainframe. The unique capability of the mainframe vis-a-vis the capability of distributed systems should be recognized in determining which services will be provided by the mainframe in the future, and which will not.

Recommendation 39. It is recommended that current efforts in the area of planning be extended and that long-range plans ultimately become an integral part of the annual budget process, involving all units of the university.

Summary

Our recommendations have addressed themselves to:
- the need for a single faculty, equally dedicated to teaching and research
- an emphasis on quality in all appointments and promotions
- a concern for a Catholic presence among the faculty
- a concern for the continued presence of members of the Holy Cross Order on the faculty, in the hall, and in the administration
- a concern for the intellectual, social, and spiritual components of student life
- the need to strengthen bonds between the alumni and the university.

From a programmatic point of view our recommendations emphasize:
- the need for a re-evaluation of the curriculum in the light of the mission of the university
- a concern for the development of graduate studies
- the need for complete reviews of each of the academic units over a period of seven years
- a desire to develop continuing education.

In addition, there are recommendations that:
- the university find and provide the necessary resources in terms of personnel, the library, research time and equipment, and facilities
- the university make a concerted effort to increase endowment for undergraduate student aid.

In essence,
- we must excel as a university in the full sense of the word, actively engaged in teaching and research
- we must maintain our Catholic identity
- we must remain conscious of and faithful to our mission in all our actions and decisions.

Statement of the Board of Trustees

On November 30, 1982, Provost Timothy O'Meara presented to the president of the university, Rev. Theodore M. Hesburgh, C.S.C., "A Report on Priorities and Commitments for Excellence (PACE) at the University of Notre Dame."

Father Hesburgh in due time forwarded the PACE Report to the board of trustees, which has gratefully received it as a thoughtful document which has been thoroughly discussed and which should stimulate much further discussion on the mission of the university and the integration of that mission into the total life of Notre Dame.

The board of trustees commends and expresses its gratitude to Professor O'Meara and to all those who participated in the discussion from which the provost's personal report to the president emanated. At this time, the board of trustees believes it would be useful and salutary to cite certain principles which are either explicit or implicit in the PACE Report and to which it wishes to subscribe. It calls these principles to the attention of the university's several constituencies, including the faculty, students, parents, alumni, friends, and benefactors.

1. The board of trustees perceives Notre Dame as a private coeducational university, Catholic in character, in its heritage, and in the values it espouses, founded by the Congregation of Holy Cross and governed by a predominantly lay board, committed to excellence in its teaching and research programs.

2. The trustees see Notre Dame as standing on the threshold of greatness. They commit themselves to marshal the intellectual and financial resources necessary for greatness in the leadership and administration of the university, in the faculty, in the student body, and in facilities.

3. The board expresses its utmost confidence in the president, provost, and other officers of the university administration, while preparing prudently and carefully for an orderly succession of leadership as exigencies require. We are also mindful of the growing excellence of the faculty and student body.

4. As a matter of deep conviction and commitment, the board seeks to reinforce Notre Dame's Catholic character. Fundamentally, this is best done by the presence of excellent Catholic scholars in sufficient numbers to maintain and deepen the traditional values and heritage of Notre Dame. The University has also traditionally been ecumenical in welcoming faculty members and students of other reli-

gious faiths to the campus community. The trustees regard the founding religious community, the Congregation of Holy Cross, as a unique source of strength and leadership in the life of university — spiritually, academically, and administratively.

5. The board of trustees reaffirms the university's commitment to academic freedom, to the principle that faculty members be outstanding as teachers as well as scholars, to the importance of a substantial liberal education component in the curriculum of the undergraduate colleges, to the centrality of theology and philosophy in a Notre Dame education, and to the traditional emphasis on a strong undergraduate program.

6. As a governing board, the trustees recognize graduate studies and research as having the greatest potential for new levels of excellence at Notre Dame. We subscribe to the proposition that strong graduate and research programs be reinforced, that there be a concentration of effort and resources in those disciplines in which Notre Dame traditionally and currently has a special strength, and that greater resources be developed for doctoral fellowships and stipends.

7. The trustees recognize continuing education as a relatively new and important dimension of Notre Dame, and they express their special interest in the development of continuing education programs for alumni.

8. The board of trustees is pleased that Notre Dame continues to attract absolutely first-rate students from every state in the union and many foreign countries. It regards the 1972 advent of coeducation as one of the most notable developments of the modern history of the university. It sees residentiality as a hallmark of a Notre Dame education and commits itself to improvement in the quality of student life. It believes that campus social and recreational facilities and programs should be commensurate with the University's residential character.

9. The trustees believe that Notre Dame should be open to qualified students of all economic circumstances. A concerted effort must be made to enlarge our resources for student financial aid.

10. The board of trustees is convinced that there is a direct correlation between the size of the university's endowment and the level of excellence of its endeavors. We seek resources for an ever-growing endowment. We look foward to the day when every senior faculty position will be endowed and when financial assistance is available to all students according to the measure of their need. The trustees recognize that the university must continue to provide library, computer, and all other reources needed for serious scholarhsip.

11. While higher education centers around the relationship of professor and student, it must take place in a physical setting. Although undergraduate enrollment is expected to remain stable at present levels, the board of trustees supports programs of construction and renovation which strengthen Notre Dame in its academic, religious, residential, and athletic dimensions to the extent that resources are available.

12. As trustees, we are pleased to note the growing interest in the fine arts at Notre Dame as reflected in the Departments of Art and Music and the Snite Museum of Art. We believe that a university should be no less a place of beauty than a focus on truth and goodness.

13. The trustees wish to record their support of Notre Dame's athletic program in its scope, quality, and integrity. We are proud of the university's athletic tradition and accomplishments and endorse the values of athletic participation by young men and women.

Finally, we look to the future of Notre Dame with the greatest optimism and confidence. We believe that the university has no less than a providential mission to serve the nation, the world, and the Church. The board of trustees, individually and collectively, pledges its commitment and support of that mission.

Sources

Bowen, W. G. *Graduate Education in the Arts and Sciences: Prospects for the Future.* Princeton, N.J.: Princeton University Press, 1981.

Boyer, E. L. and Heckinger, F. M. *Higher Learning in the Nation's Service.* New York: Carnegie Foundation, 1981.

Carnegie Council on Policy Studies in Higher Education. *Three Thousand Futures.* San Francisco: Jossey-Bass, 1980.

Dougherty, J. P., Fitzgerald, D., Langan, T., and Schmitz, K. "The Secularization of Western Culture and the Catholic College and University." *Current Issues in Catholic Higher Education,* 1981, 2 (1), 7–23.

Levine, A. *When Dreams and Heroes Died.* San Francisco: Jossey-Bass, 1980.

Newman, J. H. *The Idea of a University.* South Bend, Ind.: University of Notre Dame Press, 1982.

Schlereth, T. J. *The University of Notre Dame: A Portrait of Its History and Campus.* South Bend, Ind.: University of Notre Dame Press, 1976.

Sloan Commission. *A Program for Renewed Partnership.* Cambridge, Mass.: Ballinger, 1980.

Stadtman, V. A. *Academic Adaptations.* San Francisco: Jossey-Bass, 1980.

Timothy O'Meara is provost of the University of Notre Dame.

Index

A

Accountability, and reallocation, 60
American Association of University Professors, 86
Anandam, K., 2, 63–75
Anderson, K. O., $3n$
Aquinas College, and reduction in size, 44
Argus Panoptes, 8

B

Baker, T. S., $3n$
Baldwin, R. G., 38
Bean, J. P., $3n$
Birmingham-Southern College, participatory leadership at, 23–24, 26
Blackburn, R. T., 38
Bloom, B. S., 74, 75
Bowen, H. R., 44, 47, 49, 50, 51, 52–54, 61
Bowen, W. G., 99
Bowen, Z., $3n$
Boyer, E. L., 99
Brakeman, L., 38
Brooks, G. E., 2, 3–5
Brown, D. G., 1–2
Brown University, academic direction at, 80, 81
Budgeting, and quality, 49–62
Burns, G. P., 17

C

Canada, and collaborative technology, 72
Career redirection, and faculty development, 36–37
Carnegie Council on Policy Studies in Higher Education, 99
Caruso, A. C., 2, 43–47
Centrality, and program retrenchment, 54–55
Change, and participatory leadership, 25–28
Chief administrative officers (CAOs): and academic health, 13–14; analysis

of views of, 7–17; aphorisms and maxims for, 3–5; campus viewed by, 12–14; characteristics of, 12–13; and faculty development, 31–38; and faculty leadership, 39–42; and governance, 43–47; and long-range planning, 85–99; and missions, 77–83; national view of, 15–16; oblique view by, 11–12; and participatory leadership, 19–30; peers viewed by, 10–11; and reallocation of resources, 49–62; reviews by, 16–17; subordinates viewed by, 9–10; superiors viewed by, 8–9; systemwide view of, 14–15; and technologies, 63–75
Cohen, M. D., 17
Collegiality, and reallocation, 49, 53, 58, 60–61
Colorado, University of, and reallocation of resources, 43–44
Computers. *See* Technologies
Cost, and program retrenchment, 56–57

D

Darrow, C. N., 38
Decision making: characteristics of, in governance, 45–46; in leadership, 19, 21, 23
Delegation, in participatory leadership, 27
Demand, and program retrenchments, 55–56
Departmental chairs, and faculty development, 36
Dougherty, J. P., 99
Douglass, S. K., 51, 61
Dyer, F. C., 17
Dyer, J. M., 17

E

Eble, K. E., 17
Eddy, M. S., 59, 61
Edgerton, R., 38
Eliot, C. W., 1

104

U

United Kingdom, and collaborative technology, 72

V

Voelkel, R. T., $3n$

W

Walker, D. E., 17

Waterman, R. H., Jr., 19, 21, 23, 28–29
Wolverton, R. E., 2, 7–17
Wong, F. F., $3n$

Y

Young, C. A., 2, 49–62

Z

Zeisel, M., 38